cirencester
college
a beacon college

endorsed for

BTEC

D0255727

REVISE BTEC

Health and Social Care

Unit 1 Human Lifespan Development

Unit 9 Healthy Living

REVISION GUIDE

cirencester
college
a beacon college

Series Consultant: Harry Smith

Authors: Brenda Baker and Elizabeth Haworth

A note from the publisher

In order to ensure that this resource offers high-quality support for the associated Pearson qualification, it has been through a review process by the awarding body. This process confirms that; this resource fully covers the teaching and learning content of the specification or part of a specification at which it is aimed. It also confirms that it demonstrates an appropriate balance between the development of subject skills, knowledge and understanding, in addition to preparation for assessment.

Endorsement does not cover any guidance on assessment activities or processes (e.g. practice questions or advice on how to answer assessment questions), included in the resource nor does it prescribe any particular approach to the teaching or delivery of a related course.

While the publishers have made every attempt to ensure that advice on the qualification and its assessment is accurate, the official specification and associated assessment guidance materials are the only authoritative source of information and should always be referred to for definitive guidance.

Pearson examiners have not contributed to any sections in this resource relevant to examination papers for which they have responsibility.

Examiners will not use endorsed resources as a source of material for any assessment set by Pearson.

Endorsement of a resource does not mean that the resource is required to achieve this Pearson qualification, nor does it mean that it is the only suitable material available to support the qualification, and any resource lists produced by the awarding body shall include this and other appropriate resources.

For the full range of GCSE, **BTEC and AS/A Level** www.pearsonschools.

ALWAYS LEARNING

PEARSON

Published by Pearson Education Limited, 80 Strand, London, WC2R 0RL.

www.pearsonschoolsandfecolleges.co.uk

Copies of official specifications for all Pearson qualifications may be found on the website: www.edexcel.com

Text © Pearson Education Limited 2014
Typeset by Tech-Set Ltd, Gateshead
Original illustrations © Pearson Education Limited
Cover photo/illustration by Miriam Sturdee

The rights of Brenda Baker and Elizabeth Haworth to be identified as authors of this work have been asserted by them in accordance with the Copyright, Designs and Patents Act 1988.

First published 2014

17 16
10 9 8 7 6 5 4 3

British Library Cataloguing in Publication Data
A catalogue record for this book is available from the British Library

ISBN 978 1 4469 0981 2

Printed in Slovakia by Neografia

Acknowledgements
The publisher would like to thank the following for their kind permission to reproduce their photographs:
(Key: b-bottom; c-centre; l-left; r-right; t-top)

DK Images: Dave King 21tl; **Fotolia.com:** asaijdler 28bl, bit24 21bl, Christopher Dodge 28br, Ingus Evertovskis 21tr; **Veer / Corbis:** Alliance 64, CaptureLight 1, Corepics 3, haveseen 5, Monkey Business images 42, Mykola Lunov 14, naumoid 49, photosoup 28tc, stillfx 7, Vladimir Koletic 28tl
All other images © Pearson Education

Picture Research by: Susie Prescott
Every effort has been made to trace the copyright holders and we apologise in advance for any unintentional omissions. We would be pleased to insert the appropriate acknowledgement in any subsequent edition of this publication.

The author and publisher would like to thank the following organisations for their approval and permission to produce their materials:

p.22 Press release by the Trade Unions Congress: Shock rise in gender pay gap after years of slow, steady progress. Issued: 12 December 2013. **p.40** Definition of 'health': Preamble to the Constitution of the World Health Organization as adopted by the International Health Conference, New York, 19-22 June, 1946; signed on 22 July 1946 by the representatives of 61 States (Official Records of the World Health Organization, no. 2, p. 100) and entered into force on 7 April 1948. The Definition has not been amended since 1948. **p.53** Smoking, drinking and drug use among young people in England in 2012, Copyright 2013, re-used with the permission of the Health and Social Care Information Centre. All rights reserved.

A note from the publisher

In order to ensure that this resource offers high-quality support for the associated BTEC qualification, it has been through a review process by the awarding body to confirm that it fully covers the teaching and learning content of the specification or part of a specification at which it is aimed, and demonstrates an appropriate balance between the development of subject skills, knowledge and understanding, in addition to preparation for assessment.

While the publishers have made every attempt to ensure that advice on the qualification and its assessment is accurate, the official specification and associated assessment guidance materials are the only authoritative source of information and should always be referred to for definitive guidance.

BTEC examiners have not contributed to any sections in this resource relevant to examination papers for which they have responsibility.

No material from an endorsed book will be used verbatim in any assessment set by BTEC.

Endorsement of a book does not mean that the book is required to achieve this BTEC qualification, nor does it mean that it is the only suitable material available to support the qualification, and any resource lists produced by the awarding body shall include this and other appropriate resources.

Contents

This book covers the externally assessed units in the BTEC Level 1/Level 2 First in Health and Social Care qualification.

1-to-1 page match with the BTEC First in Health and Social Care Revision Workbook ISBN 978-1-4469-0982-9

- -

Pearson publishes Sample Assessment Material and the Specification on its website. That is the official content, and this book should be used in conjunction with it. The questions in the *Now try this* sections have been written to help you practise every topic in the book. Remember: the real test questions may not look like this.

The six life stages

In the human lifespan, there are six life stages. You should know the names of each life stage and what ages each stage covers.

1 Infancy (0-2 years)

3 Adolescence (9-18 years)

5 Middle adulthood (46-65 years)

0 ————————— Age in years ————————— 100

Early childhood (3-8 years)

2

Early adulthood (19-45 years)

4

Later adulthood (65+ years)

6

Worked example

Ewan is 15 years old. He lives at home with his family and goes to the local school. He enjoys playing chess in his spare time.

Which life stage is Ewan in? **(1 mark)**

A ☐ Early adulthood

B ☐ Infancy

C ☑ Adolescence

D ☐ Middle adulthood

Make sure you **learn** the exact age ranges for each of the six life stages. In your test you might need to choose the correct life stage for a person of a given age.

Now try this

This photo shows Jake with his grandparents.

Complete these sentences to show the current life stage of each person. **(3 marks)**

(a) Angie is in the ……………………… life stage.

(b) Jake is in the ……………………… life stage.

(c) Geoff is in the ……………………… life stage.

Geoff is 67 years old

Angie is 59 years old

Jake is 6 years old

Aspects of development

GROWTH and DEVELOPMENT are changes that individuals experience through the life stages. There are FOUR key aspects of growth and development.

1 Physical development – growth and other physical changes that happen to our body throughout life

2 Intellectual/cognitive development – the development of language, memory and thinking skills

3 Emotional development – the ability to cope with feelings about ourselves and towards others

4 Social development – the ability to form friendships and relationships and to learn to be independent

---

Worked example

Nadeem was bullied in his last year at school. He is due to start college soon, but is worried because he now finds it difficult to socialise with other young people.

Identify **two** aspects of Nadeem's development that have been most affected by bullying.   **(2 marks)**

1 His emotional development.

2 His social development.

PIES

The word PIES will help you to remember the four aspects of development:

Physical
Intellectual
Emotional
Social

Nadeem is **worried** and finds it **difficult to socialise**. This tells you that he has developed negative feelings about himself and is struggling to make friends. His **emotional** and **social** development has been **most** affected by the bullying.

Now try this

Baby Brad is 6 months old. His mother, Alexa, has taken him to the baby clinic for his six-month check-up.

The photo opposite shows him being weighed.

Which aspect of Brad's development is the nurse checking?   **(1 mark)**

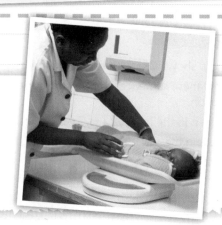

Growth and physiological change

The term growth describes an increase in height and weight. Growth continues until EARLY ADULTHOOD. The term physiological change describes the physical changes that take place throughout the life stages.

Key changes

1 Infancy/early childhood
Children grow rapidly and develop many physical skills.

2 Adolescent
The body continues to develop. There may be GROWTH SPURTS. Bodies will change as they reach SEXUAL MATURITY.

3 Young adult
The body has reached PHYSICAL MATURITY.

4 Older adult
The AGEING PROCESS begins in middle adulthood.

Worked example

Ben is 15 years old. In the last year he has grown rapidly and is now 175 cm tall. Ben is fit and active, and he is the fastest sprinter in his year group at school.

1 At what life stage will Ben reach his full height?
(1 mark)

A ☑ Early adulthood

B ☐ Infancy

C ☐ Adolescence

D ☐ Middle adulthood

2 At what life stage will Ben begin the ageing process?
(1 mark)

Ben will begin the ageing process when he reaches the middle adulthood life stage.

Key terms

GROWTH SPURTS: periods of fast growth

SEXUAL MATURITY: when an individual's reproductive organs are fully matured

PHYSICAL MATURITY: when an individual reaches their full height and the peak of physical fitness

AGEING PROCESS: by about 65, individuals will have lost some strength and muscle tone

In this answer you are only expected to identify the life stages. You don't need to identify specific ages.

Now try this

Give **one** example of physical growth and **one** example of a physiological change. **(2 marks)**

Gross motor skills

Gross motor skills allow infants to control large muscles in the body to enable them to crawl, walk and run, for example.

Hopscotch

Digging

Riding a bike

Activities that promote gross motor skils

Push-and-pull toys

Playing catch

Climbing frames

Ride-on toys

This child is using gross motor skills to help him to control his movements and kick the ball.

Stages of gross motor skills development

It is important that you know the sequence of gross motor skills development, because you will need to suggest suitable activities for infants and children of different ages.

1 Infants develop their gross motor skills from the head down.

2 They gradually control muscles in their neck and then their back so that they can roll, sit and crawl.

3 The muscles in their legs and feet develop so that they can stand and then walk.

4 and **5** In early childhood, the large muscles continue to develop to help coordination and balance.

Worked example

Explain **two** ways in which playing in the playground will help children's gross motor skills development.

(4 marks)

1 In this type of play, children will hop, run and climb. This will help them to develop strength and control because they are using the large muscles in their legs.

2 The children will develop coordination because they are using their whole body, arms and legs to help them to climb.

Just **describing** what children do in a playground – for instance, climbing – will not answer this question fully. This answer also **explains** the motor skills, such as muscle strength and coordination, that children develop as they play.

Now try this

1 Identify **two** examples of gross motor skills that infants are developing at 12 months. **(2 marks)**

2 For **each** gross motor skill, give **one** example of an activity that could be used to develop that gross motor skill.

(2 marks)

Complete the table below.

Gross motor skill	Activity

Fine motor skills

Fine motor skills allow infants and young children to control and coordinate their hands and fingers.

Examples of fine motor skills

MANIPULATING
At first, babies use their whole hand to manipulate objects. By 12 months, they are starting to use the small muscles in their fingers.

GRIPPING
By one month, babies can grasp an adult's finger. By three months, they can grasp a rattle for a short time.

HAND–EYE COORDINATION
This child is able to use the muscles in her fingers to pick up the construction piece and use her eyes to guide her finger movements.

Activities that promote fine motor skills

Knowing how children develop their fine motor skills is important, as it will help you to identify suitable activities for children of different ages.

Fine motor skill	Activity
Gripping	• Playing with a rattle • Holding a small toy • Feeding self with spoon
Manipulation	• Building with blocks • Playing with toy farm animals • Playing musical instruments
Hand–eye coordination	• Playing with jigsaw puzzles • Writing • Sewing

Writing helps to develop hand–eye coordination.

Some actions might use more than one type of fine motor skill. An alternative answer could be that Kia will use manipulation when she fastens her buttons.

Worked example

Kia is 4 years old. She is becoming independent and likes to dress herself for school.

Give **two** examples of the fine motor skills that Kia might use when dressing herself. **(2 marks)**

1 Kia will use hand–eye coordination when she fastens the buttons on her cardigan.

2 Kia will use her hands to grip when she pulls on her boots or does up the fastenings on her shoes.

Now try this

Which phrase best describes the term fine motor skills? **(1 mark)**

A ☐ The development of movement in the large muscles in arms and legs

B ☐ How development progresses from simple to more complex actions

C ☐ The development of movement of the small muscles of the fingers and hands

D ☐ How children grow and develop their physical skills

5

Physical development in adolescence

Adolescence is the life stage between the ages of 9 and 18 years.

Puberty

During adolescence, young people experience a period of change called PUBERTY. This starts when the brain releases chemicals called HORMONES.

Reaching new heights

During the adolescence life stage, a young person's height can increase rapidly over a short period of time – this is known as a growth spurt.

Changes to primary sexual characteristics

PRIMARY SEXUAL CHARACTERISTICS are present at birth. Examples include the ovaries, vagina, testes and penis. They are necessary for reproduction. During puberty, hormones cause the sexual and reproductive organs to mature.

Changes to secondary sexual characteristics

SECONDARY SEXUAL CHARACTERISTICS appear during puberty. They are caused by changes to the height and shape of the body, and distinguish the two sexes. Examples are the female breasts and facial hair for males. Secondary sexual characteristics are not necessary for reproduction.

Primary and secondary sexual characteristics

Male sexual characteristics	Female sexual characteristics
PRIMARY • Penis enlarges • Prostate gland produces secretions • Testes enlarge and produce sperm	PRIMARY • Uterus and vagina grow • Ovulation and menstrual periods begin
SECONDARY • Growth of facial hair • Growth of armpit hair/pubic hair • Increased muscle and strength • Growth spurt • Voice box (larynx) grows so the voice deepens (breaks)	SECONDARY • Enlargement of breasts • Growth of armpit hair/pubic hair • Increased fat layers under the skin • Growth spurt

Worked example

Identify **two** primary and **two** secondary sexual characteristics that a boy will develop during puberty.   **(4 marks)**

Primary sexual characteristics

1 Penis enlarges

2 Testes produce sperm

Secondary sexual characteristics

1 Voice breaks

2 Hair grows in the armpits

You may think of more examples of secondary characteristics, but this question only asks you to give **two** examples. You will not gain extra marks for listing more.

Now try this

Explain the difference between **primary** and **secondary** sexual characteristics.

(2 marks)

Physical development in adulthood

People reach physical maturity at about 19, as they reach early adulthood. During middle adulthood, they begin the ageing process.

Stages of development in adulthood

Life stage	Physical characteristics
Early adulthood	• Physically mature • Reach full height and strength • Have developed sexual characteristics and are able to reproduce • Women are at their most fertile
Middle adulthood	• Begin to show signs of ageing, such as greying hair • Begin to lose muscle tone and strength • Body shape may change with an increase in weight • Men may notice hair loss • For women menstruation ends, they are no longer able to have children
Later adulthood	• Ageing process continues with further strength and muscle loss • Stamina reduces • Mobility (gross motor skills) and dexterity (fine motor skills) become more difficult • May experience some loss of hearing and eyesight

Menopause

The MENOPAUSE is experienced by women. It can begin at any time during middle adulthood and may take several years. PHYSIOLOGICAL (or physical) changes during menopause include the gradual ending of menstruation and shrinkage of the sexual organs. Symptoms include hot flushes and night sweats.

Worked example

Peter is 69 years old. He is retired. He used to play football for a local team but now just watches rather than taking part.

Explain **two** possible effects on Peter's physical development at his life stage. **(4 marks)**

1 Peter may become tired more easily because he has less stamina.

2 He may no longer have the strength needed to play football because he has lost some of his muscle tone.

The word 'because' shows that you are explaining the effects on his physical development.

Now try this

Give **two** characteristics of physical maturity. **(2 marks)**

7

Intellectual development

Intellectual/cognitive development is about how individuals organise their ideas and make sense of the world around them.

PROBLEM SOLVING – needed to work things out and make predictions about what might happen

MORAL DEVELOPMENT – needed for reasoning and making choices about how to act towards self and others

Types of intellectual development

LANGUAGE DEVELOPMENT – essential to organise and express thoughts

MEMORY – essential for storing and recalling information

ABSTRACT THOUGHT and CREATIVE THINKING – essential for thinking and discussing things that can't be observed

Worked example

Neil is 45 years old. He works full time as a bricklayer. He has just begun a part-time photography course at his local college.

Explain **two** positive effects of attending the course on Neil's intellectual development.   **(4 marks)**

1 Neil will develop creative thinking skills, because he will need to plan ways to take and improve his photographs.

2 Neil will have to develop problem-solving skills, because he will need to work out how to use the camera and download his photographs.

When you are asked to explain something, always write in full sentences rather just than listing ideas.

Stages of intellectual development

1 Infancy and the early years are stages of rapid intellectual development.

2 Intellectual development continues throughout the life stages.

3 Thinking skills and short-term memory may decline in later adulthood.

4 Older people may experience dementia, which is an illness affecting the brain that causes memory loss.

Now try this

Marie is 65 years old and has just retired. Her job required her to come up with solutions to problems and think creatively, so she is worried that her ability to problem-solve and her memory may decline.

Which **two** of the following activities would be most effective in promoting Marie's intellectual development?

    (2 marks)

A ☐ Joining a reading group   B ☐ Meeting up with friends regularly

C ☐ Learning a foreign language   D ☐ Joining a keep-fit class

E ☐ Taking up gardening

Language development

Language development is needed for thinking and learning.

Stages of language development

Life stage	Age range	Characteristics of language development
Infancy	0–3 months	• Makes mouth movements at 6 weeks • Responds by gurgling • Cries to ask for food or comfort
	6–12 months	• Understands some words such as 'bye bye' • Makes sounds such as 'ba ba' or 'ga ga' • Can give an object when asked
	18 months	• Uses a small number of words (about six to ten) to communicate • Repeats what others say • Can follow instructions
	2 years	• Can link two words together (for example, 'mine car') • By 2 and a half years, knows about 200 words
Early childhood	3 years	• Speech is clearer • Uses simple sentences • Begins to ask questions
	4 years	• Speaks in sentences • May use incorrect form of word such as 'I goed'
	8 years	• Develops independent reading skills • Uses complex sentences • Can reason and explain
Adolescence	9–18 years	• Continues to develop vocabulary • Uses language to discuss abstract ideas; for example, using imagination to explore new ideas

Opportunities for promoting language development

Play with puppets　Watch and listen to other children　Take part in group activities (cooking or water play)　Play imaginatively (shopping or home play)　Take part in group projects　Discuss ideas

Infants need to:

Young children need to:

Adolescents need to:

Join in with action rhymes and songs　Share picture books　Share stories and rhymes　Play word games and riddles　Read a wide range of books and materials

Worked example

Make sure you read the question carefully and always check how many items the question asks you to provide.

Jack is 2 years old. He is looked after at home by his mother, Patricia. She is planning to take Jack to a playgroup for two mornings each week.

Give **two** examples of expected language development for Jack. **(2 marks)**

1 Jack will know around 50 words.

2 Jack will be linking together two words.

Now try this

Patricia hopes that the staff at the playgroup will be able to help Jack with his language skills.

Identify **two** activities that the playgroup staff could use to help Jack to develop his language skills. **(2 marks)**

Moral development

Moral development is about the values that individuals develop.

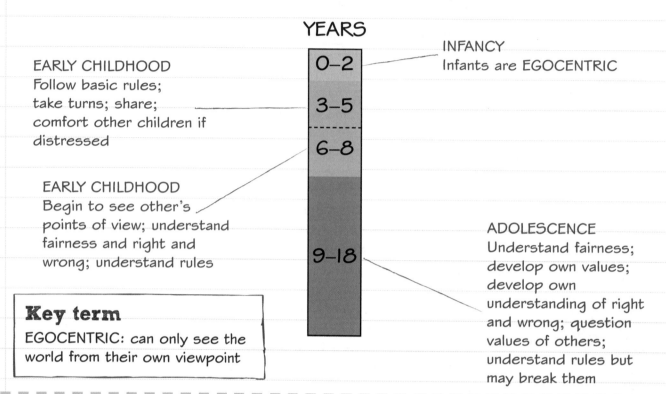

YEARS

EARLY CHILDHOOD
Follow basic rules;
take turns; share;
comfort other children if
distressed

0–2

3–5

6–8

9–18

INFANCY
Infants are EGOCENTRIC

EARLY CHILDHOOD
Begin to see other's
points of view; understand
fairness and right and
wrong; understand rules

ADOLESCENCE
Understand fairness;
develop own values;
develop own
understanding of right
and wrong; question
values of others;
understand rules but
may break them

Key term

EGOCENTRIC: can only see the
world from their own viewpoint

Understanding rules

- INFANTS (0–2 years) are not able to understand rules, but are beginning to learn how to behave by watching others.
- CHILDREN (3–8 years) can understand rules and often remind others of how they should act.
- ADOLESCENTS (9–18 years) begin to question rules that they feel are not fair.

Worked example

Identify the usual age at which children start to
recognise distress in others.   **(1 mark)**

A ☑ 3 years

B ☐ 4 years

C ☐ 6 years

D ☐ 8 years

Older children will also comfort friends
who are distressed, but this question
asks you to identify the life stage when
children **start** to do this.

You may notice that around the age of
3 years, children will try to comfort other
children or even adults who are upset.

Now try this

Ajay is 7 years old and is starting his third year of school. At the beginning of the term, his teacher asked him and
his friends to discuss and agree the rules for behaviour in the classroom.

Give **one** possible effect of discussing the class rules on Ajay's moral development.   **(1 mark)**

Emotional development

Emotional development is about the development of feelings about oneself and others.

SELF-IMAGE – how people respect and value themselves

CONTENTMENT – how happy someone is with their life

SECURITY – the feeling of safety and being loved

What is emotional development?

SELF-RESPECT – how people respect and value others

BONDING AND ATTACHMENT – the emotional bonds that a person forms with others (for example, between children and parents)

Self-image

A person's self-image may be positive or negative.

Positive self-image	Negative self-image
✓ Feels happy about personal appearance and abilities	✗ Feels unattractive or less intelligent than others
✓ Receives good feedback from others about appearance or abilities	✗ Receives negative comments from others on appearance or abilities
✓ Compares self favourably with others	✗ Compares self negatively against 'perfect' images in magazines/on TV

High self-esteem

People with high self-esteem will feel confident.

Low self-esteem

People with low self-esteem may feel worthless.

Self-esteem can be affected by:
- the attitudes of others
- family support
- success at work or school
- negative or positive things that others say.

Worked example

Rakeesh is 28 years old. He has worked in the car industry since he left school. Recently he applied for promotion. He thought he had done well at the interview, but he has not been successful.

Explain **one** possible effect of not getting the job on Rakeesh's self-esteem. **(2 marks)**

Rakeesh may have received poor feedback after the interview, which may negatively affect his self-esteem.

This learner has shown that they understand that comments from others can affect self-esteem.

Now try this

Think about different aspects of emotional development when answering this question.

Ashton is 18 months old. He is loved and well cared for.

Describe **two** possible effects of being loved and well cared for on Ashton's emotional development. **(4 marks)**

Social development

Social development is the way that individuals become INDEPENDENT and form FRIENDSHIPS and RELATIONSHIPS with others.

Building relationships

Friendships: these involve learning to value others and developing the skills needed to make friends with individuals and with groups of people.

Relationships: these involve developing the skills to interact with other people in FORMAL (for example, with colleagues at work) and INFORMAL situations (for example, within a family). They also cover intimate relationships in adulthood.

Independence: this involves doing things by oneself and making decisions without relying on others.

Promoting independence

Tasks and activities that promote independence include:

Infancy	Feeding oneself
Early childhood	Dressing oneself
Adolescence	Learning to drive
Adulthood	Starting a new job

Learning to drive gives adolescents independence.

Hilary is 43 years old and lives with her husband, Gerard. They are both teachers and are also keen tennis players. Hilary was recently involved in a car accident, which injured her back. She can no longer work or take part in sport.

Explain **two** possible effects of the accident on Hilary's social development. **(4 marks)**

1 Hilary has lost some of her independence because of her injury and will have to rely on her husband to help her with tasks.

2 Hilary will not meet as many people as she did when she was working and playing sport, so will not be able to build new relationships.

Social and emotional development

Social development is closely linked with emotional development. Some questions will require you to identify or explain the effects of both aspects of development.

This answer shows a good understanding of social development. Not only does it show an understanding of Hilary's loss of independence, but it also shows an understanding of the wider effects of not being able to take part in sports (for example, she won't meet as many people).

Identify **two** ways in which the development of independence in children can help promote their social development.
(2 marks)

Emotional and social development in infancy

Emotional and social development in infancy are very closely linked.

Emotional and social development timeline

12 months: begins to bond with other people but still very dependent on parents

2 years: can become frustrated easily and often has temper tantrums

2 years: may play alongside other children but does not share toys and activities

3 months | 12 months | 2 years

Birth | 6 months | 18 months | 2½ years

6 months: has developed strong bond with parents

18 months: plays alone but likes an adult or brother or sister to be close by

2½ years: may show jealousy towards other children

Emotional development

SECURITY is essential for positive emotional development. Infants feel secure when they:
- are looked after by a familiar carer
- are shown love
- have a routine
- are kept safe from harm.

Key term
ATTACHMENT: the bond between children and their parents and carers

This answer shows good knowledge of how infants develop **emotionally** and **socially** by explaining how Rosie may react when being looked after by an unfamiliar person.

Worked example

Carla is 31 years old and is a single mother. She has one child, Rosie, who is 11 months old.

Recently, Carla was taken ill suddenly and has to go into hospital for several weeks. Rosie is being looked after by a foster carer.

Explain **one** possible negative effect and **one** possible positive effect on Rosie's emotional and social development. **(4 marks)**

Negative effect: Rosie may become more easily distressed, because she has strong bonds with her mother and the person looking after her is not familiar to her.

Positive effect: Rosie may start to form attachments to other people and learn to become less dependent on her mother.

Now try this

Marta has a new baby, Felix, who is 2 months old. Marta has taken time off from work to look after Felix, because she knows that he is dependent on her for his needs.

Give **two** reasons why infants are dependent on their parents. **(2 marks)**

Emotional and social development in early childhood

Learning how to cope with their own feelings helps children when they begin to build friendships with other children and adults. Emotional and social development are closely linked.

Emotional development

In early childhood, children:
- are able to say how they feel
- understand if they feel happy or sad
- are learning to cope with own feelings
- are developing a mental image of themselves (self-image).

Children's self-esteem is influenced by achievements and feedback from others.

Social development

In early childhood, children:
- develop independence
- develop special friendships
- develop a wider circle of friends
- can share and take turns
- form relationships with adults other than their parents.

Children may need adults to help them to cope with their feelings.

From the age of 3 years, children can share and take turns when they play with others.

Worked example

Alisha is 7 years old. She recently started going to dance classes after school.

Give **one** possible effect on Alisha's emotional development and **one** possible effect on Alisha's social development. **(2 marks)**

Social development: Alisha will make new friends.

Emotional development: Alisha's self-esteem will be improved.

> Make sure that you give an answer for each aspect of development specified in the question.

Now try this

> Think about the importance of self-esteem, self-image or children's ability to cope with their own feelings when building friendships.

Jodie is 4 years old and is still very dependent on her mother. She is reluctant to try new things and often becomes frustrated and has tantrums. Jodie is due to start school next month.

Give **one** example of how Jodie's emotional development may affect her ability to make friends at school.

(1 mark)

Emotional and social development in adolescence

Maturing physically and sexually can have a significant effect on the emotional and social development of ADOLESCENTS. Emotional and social development is very closely linked.

Enjoying more independence and freedom

Socialising more and meeting new people

Experiencing extremes in emotions caused by hormonal changes

Experiencing feelings of insecurity and anxiety

Characteristics of emotional and social development

Developing an awareness of own sexuality

Exploring and forming own identity (self-image)

Experiencing first close and intimate relationships

During puberty, adolescents have to cope with **mood swings** as they come to terms with their own identity, changes in their appearance and sexual maturity.

Worked example

James is 15 years old. Last year, James's dad left his mum and him, and now lives in another town. James is upset, as he used to go to sports events with his dad but now only sees him occasionally. Shortly after his dad left, James received some exam results that were disappointing. James is worried that he may not achieve the GCSE results he needs to go to college.

Assess how the changes and events in James's life may affect his emotional and social development. **(8 marks)**

James may feel that his dad left because of him. This may cause him to feel guilty and anxious. The result could be that James will develop a negative self-image. James will lose his sense of security, because his father is no longer there to care for him and spend time with him. This could cause anxiety... Not seeing his father could also affect his relationship with him in the future...

All the information you need for a question like this can be found in the case study.

This is only a partial answer. Have a go at finishing it below.

This answer looks at both **emotional** and **social** development. It refers to the case study and shows an understanding of how James's life stage will make dealing with these events more difficult.

Now try this

Refer back to the case study about James to answer this question.

Identify **four** further effects on James's emotional and social development. **(4 marks)**

15

Emotional and social development in adulthood

EARLY ADULTHOOD ①

EMOTIONAL
- Develop close and intimate relationships with others
- May have children and develop strong bonds with them

SOCIAL
- May have an active social life
- May meet new friends through leisure activities and work

MIDDLE ADULTHOOD ②

Three stages of development

EMOTIONAL
- May feel more contented as they have fewer family and work commitments
- Are usually retired so have more leisure time to spend with family and friends
- Friends or partners may die
- Loss of friends/partners can result in anxiety and insecurity

SOCIAL
- If physically active, they may have a busy social life with friends and family
- As they get older or less mobile they may not have much contact with others

LATER ADULTHOOD ③

EMOTIONAL
- May have difficulty coming to terms with ageing
- Children may leave home, which can affect emotions
- Menopause: female hormone changes can cause irritability and difficulty in coping with changing emotions

SOCIAL
- Their children may have grown up so there is more time to try out new social /leisure activities and build new relationships

---

Worked example

Nisha is 72 years old and lives alone. She does not have children, but has many friends. A few months ago, Nisha's arthritis got much worse and she can no longer drive. She even finds walking difficult.

1 Give **one** example of how the change in Nisha's mobility may affect her social development. **(1 mark)**

Nisha will not be able to travel easily to meet with friends to socialise.

2 Give **one** example of how Nisha's friends could support her social development. **(1 mark)**

Nisha's friends could visit her regularly at home.

Other factors affecting social and emotional development
- Bereavement
- Health
- Mobility
- Support of family and friends

This question only asks how Nisha's health and lack of mobility may affect her **social** development. However, you may also be asked about how these things might affect her **emotional** development.

Now try this

Anita is 27 years old. She lives with her partner Eryk. They do not have children. Eryk recently got a new job, which has meant that the couple have had to move away from friends and family. Anita had to leave her job and is now unemployed and stays at home.

Explain **two** negative effects of moving house on Anita's emotional and social development. **(4 marks)**

This question asks you to 'explain' so you need to extend your answer. Do not just say **how** Anita's development is affected, but give reasons as to **why**.

Genetic inheritance

Genetic inheritance is a physical factor that affects human growth and development.

What is genetic inheritance?

Genetic inheritance is the passing of genes from parents to children. The genes that are passed on by parents influence a person's physical features and characteristics.

Genetic characteristics

Children may inherit the following physical characteristics from their parents:

- height
- skin colour
- hair and eye colour.

Genetic characteristics can also affect emotional and social development, because they influence a person's self-image.

Genetic disorders

Genetic disorders are health conditions that are passed from parents to their children through their genes. They include:

- Down's syndrome
- sickle cell anaemia
- cystic fibrosis.

Genetic disorders may affect not only health and physical development but also intellectual, social or emotional development.

EMOTIONAL DEVELOPMENT – how people picture themselves and their feelings of wellbeing and security

PHYSICAL DEVELOPMENT – restricting or slowing growth, mobility and effects on physiological change

INTELLECTUAL DEVELOPMENT – effects on learning, thinking skills and memory as a result of a learning disorder or missing time at school because of frequent ill-health

Influence of genetic inheritance

SOCIAL DEVELOPMENT – may affect opportunities or an individual's ability to build friendships and relationships and become independent

---

Worked example

Ade is 6 years old and has sickle cell anaemia. Most of the time he feels well, but when he has an episode of sickle cell, he cannot go to school or out to play. He feels a lot of pain and has difficulty breathing.

Identify **two** possible effects that Ade's illness might have on his development. **(2 marks)**

1 Ade is missing school, which could affect his learning.

2 Ade's social development may be affected as he will not be able to play with friends when he has an episode.

Down's syndrome is an example of a genetically inherited condition.

Now try this

Identify **two** ways in which genetic inheritance may affect development. **(2 marks)**

Lifestyle choices

The lifestyle choices we make can affect all aspects of growth and development.

DIET
A healthy diet:
- contains nutrients needed for growth and development
- improves body image (for example, healthy weight and skin).

An unhealthy diet can:
- lead to weight gain, putting pressure on joints
- cause illnesses (for example, diabetes and heart disease).

ALCOHOL
- May reduce judgement/ ability to make decisions
- May negatively affect relationships.

SMOKING
- Can cause illness and disease
- May affect the growth of an unborn baby
- May cause social isolation (for example, smoking may not be considered acceptable).

Lifestyle choices

EXERCISE
Regular exercise:
- strengthens muscles and joints
- improves mobility and stamina
- helps prevent illness/disease
- improves mood.

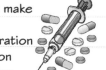

Lack of exercise may:
- reduce stamina and strength
- reduce mobility
- affect mental health negatively.

DRUGS
- Can cause illness and disease, such as problems with the heart and kidneys
- May reduce judgement/ability to make decisions
- May affect memory and concentration
- May cause anxiety and depression
- May negatively affect relationships
- May cause infertility in women.

Worked example

Alice is 27 years old and works full time as a health care assistant. Until recently she lived with her partner, Matt, but then they separated. Alice has started using drugs when she goes out with friends.

Discuss how using drugs may affect Alice's overall development.

(8 marks)

Taking drugs may affect Alice's health, causing problems with her heart or kidneys. Drugs may affect her production of hormones and cause her to become infertile so she will be unable to have children later. Although drugs may make her feel happier at the time, she is likely to feel more anxious afterwards and may become depressed. Feeling that she needs to use drugs may make her less contented. Alice's ability to ...

This is only a partial answer because it only relates to Alice's physical and emotional development.

You will need to cover all types of development and ensure you show **both sides** of the discussion. For example, you could discuss how taking drugs allows Alice to feel more independent and in control of her own life.

Now try this

Refer back to the case study about Alice to answer this question.

Assess **two** further effects that taking drugs may have on Alice's cognitive and social development. **(4 marks)**

When a question asks you to consider all aspects of a person's development, remember **PIES**. This will help you to write about all the aspects – physical, intellectual, emotional and social.

Illness and disease

This table shows some of the possible negative effects of illness and disease on development.

PHYSICAL	(X)	• May affect the rate of growth in infancy and childhood • May slow physiological change during puberty • May affect the development of fine motor skills and gross motor skills in infants and children • May restrict mobility
INTELLECTUAL	(X)	• May affect learning if school or college is missed • May lead to difficulties in creative thinking/problem solving • May affect memory and concentration
EMOTIONAL	(X)	• May lead to negative self-image • May lower self-esteem (for example, if it prevents someone from achieving their goals) • May cause isolation (for example, if mobility prevents someone from going out)
SOCIAL	(X)	• May cause loss of independence • May limit opportunities to socialise • May hinder development of relationships

Worked example

Clive is 50 years old and he recently had a heart attack. He has been discharged from hospital and is now at home. However, the doctor has told him that he must take it easy from now on. This has meant that Clive has had to give up his job as a lorry driver.

Explain **two** possible effects of Clive's illness on his development.
(4 marks)

1 Clive may have a negative self-image as he can no longer work.

2 Clive's strength and muscle tone is likely to be reduced as he is less active.

This answer identifies one effect relating to Clive's **emotional** development and one relating to his **physical** development. Other answers relating to Clive's intellectual and social development could include:
• Clive's memory may worsen, as he is not using his thinking skills as much
• Clive may not get out and socialise as much, so will not be building new relationships.

Now try this

Jamie is 9 years old. He has diabetes and so has needed to spend time in hospital. Jamie's mum is concerned about his lack of progress in his maths and English lessons compared with his friends.

Identify the **most** likely reason for Jamie's intellectual development to be delayed.   **(1 mark)**

Put a cross in **one** box to indicate your answer.

A ☐ He cannot go out to play with friends

B ☐ He has missed time at school

C ☐ He lacks confidence in his ability

D ☐ He sometimes feels isolated

The influence of play

Play is essential for all aspects of children's development.

Play in infancy and childhood

- Play influences physical, intellectual, emotional and social development.
- Infants start to play from the first few months of life.
- Infants and children enjoy playing both indoors and outdoors.
- Play can be SOLITARY or SOCIAL:
  - infants take part in solitary play
  - children, from the age of 3, take part in social play.

Solitary and social play

Solitary play is play that children do on their own, for example:
- painting
- playing with play dough
- playing with cuddly toys.

Social play is play that children take part in with others, for example:
- ball games
- playing shop
- dressing up and home corner.

How play influences development

Development	Aspect of development	Example of play activity
Physical	Fine motor skills	Painting, puzzles, construction
	Gross motor skills	Climbing frame, cycling, playing ball
Intellectual	Language, creative thinking, problem solving, memory, concentration	Shape sorting, puzzles, matching games, action songs
Emotional	Self-esteem, contentment	Painting, play dough, musical instruments, drama
Social	Sharing, making friends, independence	Home corner, playing shop, cooking, water play

Worked example

Which type of development are wheeled toys **most** important for? **(1 mark)**

A ☑ Physical development

B ☐ Intellectual development

C ☐ Emotional development

D ☐ Social development

Although this type of play may also help other areas of development, it is **most** important for a child's gross motor skills. Physical development is therefore the correct answer.

Looking back at pages 2–16 about the different aspects of development may help you to answer this question.

Now try this

At Little Stars nursery, there is a hospital corner where children aged 3 to 4 years old can play doctors and nurses. There are dressing-up clothes and toy instruments for the children to use.

Give **two** possible effects of taking part in hospital play on the children's development. **(2 marks)**

Culture

How culture influences development

Development is influenced by culture –
the community in which people live and
their beliefs (such as religious
or spiritual).

Community and beliefs can influence:
- the way people behave
- the way people dress
- what people can eat
- people's values.

Observant Jews cannot
eat pork or shellfish.

Positive effects

✓ People share the same values,
beliefs and religion.

✓ People feel accepted and are
supported by others.

✓ People feel valued by others
because of their values, beliefs and
religion.

This leads to positive self-esteem, and
promotes growth and development.

Negative effects

✗ People are discriminated against
because of their values, beliefs or
religion.

✗ People feel excluded because of their
values, beliefs or religion.

✗ A person's culture is ignored or not
understood.

This can lead to poor self-esteem and
possibly social isolation.

Worked example

Aamilah is a 72-year-old Muslim woman. Recently she has been ill and has been unable to care for herself. The
district nurse organised for meals to be delivered to Aamilah each day. Unfortunately, some of the meals have
contained foods that she cannot eat for religious reasons.

Explain **one** reason how a lack of understanding of Aamilah's religion may have a negative effect on her
development.   **(2 marks)**

Aamilah may not feel valued if she is not asked about her dietary needs, and this may
affect her emotional development.

Now try this

Amy, aged 27, lives with her husband Tim in a small village.
There is a strong feeling of community within the village and
there are many social events. Unfortunately, because of Tim's
work, Amy and Tim will soon be moving to a large city where
they do not know anyone.

Give **two** examples of possible effects of the move on Amy's
growth and development.   **(2 marks)**

When asked to give or explain
two effects, try to include
different aspects of growth
and development (for example,
social and emotional).

Gender

Gender INEQUALITIES can impact on a person's growth and development.

Traditional gender roles

Traditionally, men went out to work and women stayed at home to raise the children.

GENDER ROLES of men and women have changed considerably in recent decades.

Now both men and women go out to work and they share the responsibilities of raising children. There is also more equality of opportunities.

Key terms

GENDER ROLE: a role that is determined by a person's gender

DISCRIMINATION: unfair treatment (e.g. on the basis of gender, age or race)

Historically, there have been FOUR main types of gender inequality.

 Employment

Some jobs tend to attract more men (for example, engineering) and some attract more women (for example, nursing). In some types of work women are less likely to achieve promotion to higher level jobs (for example, managing directors).

 Pay

Research by the Trade Union Congress shows that there is still a gap between the level of pay for men and women, with men earning higher rates of pay across major occupations (Source: TUC, 2013).

 Expectations

There may be different expectations about people's skills and characteristics based on their gender (for example, that women are more caring and creative, and men are more practical).

 Social inequality

Gender may affect how you are treated, leading to social inequality and DISCRIMINATION.

For example, people may be excluded from a group because of their gender.

Worked example

Gender equality of pay is improving.

Amelia is 9 years old. She asked to play football with the boys at playtime. The boys told her that she wouldn't be able to pass the ball properly because she was a girl.

Explain **two** possible effects on Amelia's growth and development of being excluded from the game. **(4 marks)**

1 Amelia will not develop her gross motor skills and coordination if she does not take part in sport.

2 Amelia may develop a negative self-image because she may think that she isn't as good at football as the boys are.

Daily News

WOMEN WIN EQUAL PAY COMPENSATION

You will be given space on the paper to write your answer. This will indicate the amount of information you need to give.

Now try this

Pawel has worked with children for eight years. He applied for a promotion to the role of manager at the nursery school where he works. He thought he had done well at the interview. However, although he had more experience and was better qualified than the other candidates, he did not get the job.

Explain **two** possible effects of not getting the manager role on Pawel's development. **(4 marks)**

Role models and social isolation

Development may be affected by ROLE MODELS and opportunities to interact with others.

Role models

Children and young people learn by copying the behaviour of others – these are role models.

- Copying role models may have a positive or negative influence on lifestyle choices.
- Role models can also affect how people see themselves.
- Role models can have a direct influence on development.

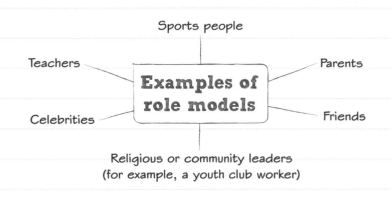

Examples of role models

- Sports people
- Teachers
- Parents
- Celebrities
- Friends
- Religious or community leaders (for example, a youth club worker)

Social isolation

Social isolation is when people do not have regular contact with others. This may be because they:

- live alone
- are unemployed
- do not have access to social situations
- are not able to easily leave their home because of illness or disease
- are discriminated against and/or are excluded.

Effects of social isolation

- May lose the ability to build new friendships and relationships
- May feel insecure and lack contentment
- May experience memory loss and recall
- May experience stress and anxiety because there is no one to share their worries with
- May adopt a negative lifestyle such as starting smoking or drinking alcohol

Worked example

Which aspect of emotional development is likely to be **most** affected by celebrity role models? **(1 mark)**

A ☐ Security

B ☐ Attachment

C ☑ Self-image

D ☐ Self-esteem

This answer correctly indicates that self-image is likely to be **most** affected. This is because young people often compare themselves with their favourite celebrity.

Now try this

Wardell is 58 years old and lives alone after his divorce. Recently, he was made redundant from his job as an IT consultant. As he isn't earning, he has little money to go out and socialise with friends.

Give **two** possible effects of not being able to socialise on Wardell's development. **(2 marks)**

This question asks you to **give** effects, so you do not need to go on to explain the reasons.

Economic factors

EMPLOYMENT STATUS – the type of work (manual or non-manual) someone does, whether it is full-time or part-time and their job security

INCOME/WEALTH – the level of income or amount of personal wealth a person has

Economic influences on development

OCCUPATION – whether a person is employed or unemployed, at school/college or in training

Positive and negative economic effects

Development	Positive effects	Negative effects
Physical	✓ • Manual jobs may improve muscle tone and stamina. • A higher income may result in better health as a result of better housing conditions and diet.	✗ • Manual jobs can cause injury and muscular and skeletal problems. • Low wages can impact on lifestyle (for example, diet), which may lead to poor health.
Intellectual	✓ • Being in work, education or training encourages development of creative thinking and problem-solving skills.	✗ • Not working (for example, retirement) or not being in education may cause worsening of memory.
Emotional	✓ • Being in work, education or training can improve self-esteem. • High-status jobs can improve self-image. • A secure job income can lead to contentment.	✗ • Unemployment, low-status jobs or low income can result in anxiety and low self-esteem. • Family relationships can suffer because of financial worries.
Social	✓ • Being in work, school or training provides opportunities for building friendships and relationships. • A higher income allows greater independence.	✗ • Unemployment or not being in education or training reduces the opportunity to build relationships. • A low income restricts opportunity for socialising.

Worked example

Kareem and his partner Angelika have three children under 6 years old. Angelika does not work. Kareem works as a security guard. He enjoys his job but only earns the minimum wage.

Explain **one** possible positive and **one** possible negative effect of Kareem's employment on his emotional development. **(4 marks)**

Positive: Kareem may have good self-esteem, as he enjoys his job.

Negative: He may feel stressed because his low wage needs to pay for all the family's needs, such as housing and food.

At first it may appear that there might only be negative effects on Kareem's emotional development. However, by looking more closely, you can find clues to more positive effects. For example, Kareem gets satisfaction out of his job even though having a low wage may cause him stress.

Now try this

Explain **two** possible effects of a person's occupational status on their emotional development. **(4 marks)**

Physical environment

ENVIRONMENTAL factors, such as housing conditions and the area in which people live, may also affect their growth and development.

Poor housing conditions

Condition	Effect
Damp conditions	• Breathing problems • Asthma
Overcrowding	• Anxiety/depression • Stress from noise levels
Lack of open spaces	• Lack of exercise
Cold living conditions/lack of heating	• Poor health (for example, illnesses such as colds and heart disease). In vulnerable people these illnesses can lead to death.

Pollution can cause **respiratory problems**, such as asthma, and other diseases, such as cancer and heart disease. The effects of pollution are greater for infants, older people and those who are ill.

Effects of pollution on health

Worked example

Mada and Jabir Hussain are married and live in a city. They rent a one-bedroom flat on a large estate close to a motorway. There are few open spaces around the estate. The flat is damp. Mada and Jabir are expecting a baby next month.

Explain the possible negative effects of the physical environment on the new baby's **physical** and **emotional** development. **(4 marks)**

Physical: The new baby may develop asthma as it grows up, because of pollution from the motorway and the damp conditions in the flat.

Emotional: The baby may find it more difficult to bond with Mada and Jabir because it may sense the stress and anxiety the parents are feeling as a result of poor housing conditions.

When looking at case studies about families, you may need to think about how life events may affect **all** members of the family. For instance, an unexpected event can cause stress for a person's partner and children.

The stress caused to parents because of the physical environment can have a significant impact on their children.

Now try this

Len is 67 years old and lives in a small flat in a very busy part of London. He has a good diet and has never smoked. However, Len has a respiratory disease called chronic bronchitis.

What is the **most** likely cause of Len's chronic bronchitis? **(1 mark)**

Put a cross in **one** box to indicate your answer.

A ☐ Len has one small heater in his flat

B ☐ Len does not have access to open spaces

C ☐ Len lives next to a very busy main road

D ☐ Len suffers a lot of noise from neighbours' flats

Family relationships

Strong family bonds are essential for positive growth and development.

The importance of family relationships

Family relationships provide:

- acceptance – unconditional acceptance of someone for who they are regardless of, for example, their lifestyle
- love – providing for all needs – physical, intellectual, emotional and social
- support – helping to prepare for expected life events and providing support during times of need (for example, unexpected life events)
- attachment – providing security.

Children in care

Children in care may experience:

- a loss of self-identity because they have not developed their family identity
- difficulty in forming strong attachments because their main carer changes
- difficulty in building relationships because they have not had the love of parents
- discrimination and stigma, which affect self-esteem.

Positive family relationships

Positive family relationships may result in:

- ✓ positive self-image
- ✓ high self-esteem
- ✓ a feeling of contentment
- ✓ the ability to build positive relationships with others outside of the family
- ✓ independence
- ✓ confidence.

Negative family relationships

A breakdown in family relationships may result in:

- ✗ negative self-image
- ✗ low self-esteem
- ✗ difficulty in building relationships with people outside of the family
- ✗ a lack of independence
- ✗ difficulty in controlling emotions.

Worked example

Bobby lives with his mum, stepdad and grandma. He sees his dad every weekend and speaks to him on the phone most nights. He is looking forward to starting school in September.

Explain **one** possible effect of positive family relationships on Bobby's emotional and social development.   **(2 marks)**

Bobby will be able to build friendships more easily because he has secure attachments at home.

Emotional and social development are closely linked. As Bobby has strong attachments with his family, he will be better able to build relationships with the new people he meets at school.

Now try this

Debbie is 22 years old. She has just informed her parents that she has decided to live with her partner Anika, who is 37 years old, and that they are planning a civil partnership. Debbie has always had a close positive relationship with her parents, and they have accepted her new relationship.

Give **two** examples of positive effects of unconditional acceptance by her parents on Debbie's emotional development.   **(2 marks)**

Friendships and relationships

Friendships and relationships can shape human growth and development.

Friendship patterns and relationships with partners

Friendship/relationship	Characteristics/benefits
Close friendships	• From the age of 3 years, children start to develop special friendships. • These make people feel SECURE and CONFIDENT. • They also promote INDEPENDENCE and SELF-ESTEEM.
Friendships with a wider group of friends	• As children widen their circle of friends, they become more confident and independent. • Adolescents are greatly influenced by the views of their friends, which may affect their SELF-IMAGE. • These continue to be important in adulthood for positive emotional and social development.
Formal relationships	• These may be relationships formed between colleagues at work or between teacher and pupil. • Getting on well with others in formal situations is important for self-image and self-esteem.
Informal relationships	• Good family relationships lead to HAPPINESS and CONTENTMENT. • Good relationships within the family help teach children how to build relationships with other people as they get older.
Intimate relationships	• These may begin in adolescence. • They continue into later adulthood and are important for SECURITY and self-image.

Worked example

Heidi met Rory when they were at college. They have now been in a relationship for 15 years. Two months ago, Rory met someone else and has decided to leave Heidi.

Explain **two** possible effects of the breakdown of their relationship on Heidi's emotional and social development. **(4 marks)**

1 Heidi may have difficulty building new relationships, because she may not be able to trust anyone in the future.

2 Heidi may have low self-image, because she may compare herself with Rory's new partner.

This learner has given two **realistic** examples and has explained the reason for each effect. These are both negative effects. The learner could have given a positive effect, explaining that Heidi may develop more independence.

Now try this

Nathan is 3 years old. He has just started school and enjoys playing with other children. He has a best friend called Nakeesh.

Give **two** possible effects of building friendships at school on Nathan's growth and development. **(2 marks)**

Stress

There are many reasons for stress. It can affect all aspects of development.

Possible effects of stress

EMOTIONAL
- May cause negative self-image
- May cause low self-esteem
- May result in feeling less secure
- May cause breakdown of attachments

SOCIAL
- May make forming friendships and relationships difficult
- May cause intimate relationships to break down
- May have less confidence in own ability
- May cause a loss of independence

Possible effects of stress

PHYSICAL
- Slows physical growth in children
- Delays the onset of puberty
- Speeds up the onset of the ageing process
- Can result in unhealthy eating, causing weight loss or gain

INTELLECTUAL
- Reduces the ability to think creatively
- Reduces the ability to problem solve
- Reduces concentration and memory

Worked example

Kira is 15 years old. She is studying for her GCSEs. She feels very stressed and anxious, because she has recently been the victim of cyber-bullying. One of her friends has posted unkind things about her on a social media website.

Evaluate the possible effects of stress on Kira's overall development.

(8 marks)

If a question asks you to evaluate **all** aspects of development, you must make sure that you cover them all to fully answer the question.

Stress may affect Kira's diet. She may comfort-eat, which might cause her to put on weight, or she may feel that she cannot eat, so may lose weight and become ill. Kira may find that she cannot concentrate on her studies because she is thinking about what has happened, so her learning may be affected. Her schoolwork might also be affected as she will be unable to solve problems as well or think creatively about her work.

She may have developed a negative self-image as a result of the unkind comments made about her on the social media website, so she may develop low self-esteem. This low self-esteem will also affect her social development as adolescence is a time when young people usually socialise more and become more independent. As she was bullied by someone she thought was a friend, she may have lost trust in others. This might mean that the friendships she has maintained will break down and she will also be more reluctant to go out to socialise and develop new friendships.

This answer covers all the possible effects on **physical**, **intellectual**, **emotional** and **social** development. It refers to the information given in the case study and relates the answer to Kira's particular situation. The answer also **evaluates** the effects and does not just explain. For instance, it explains that Kira's learning might be slowed, as she may not be able to concentrate because she is thinking about what happened.

Now try this

Identify **two** physical effects of stress.

(2 marks)

Expected life events 1

Expected life events are events that happen to most people during the course of their life.

There are some expected life events that are likely to happen to most people – for example, starting school and work.

Other events, such as marriage or parenthood, will also happen for most people but may not happen for everyone.

Events, such as moving or owning a house, may happen a bit later for some people.

Marriage or entering a civil partnership is an **expected life event**.

Some of the events that might be expected to happen in life.

(signpost labels: Leaving school · Starting school · Moving house/area · Starting a new job · Living with a partner · Marriage/civil partnership · Becoming a parent · Retirement)

Miranda is 25 years old. Miranda has worked in a bank since she left school at 18. She lives with her partner Gary.

Identify **two** expected life events that Miranda has experienced.   **(2 marks)**

A ☐ Getting married

B ☑ Moving in with a partner

C ☑ Getting a job

D ☐ Becoming a parent

E ☐ Starting university

This learner has used the information in the case study to correctly identify **two** expected life events that Miranda has experienced.

Now try this

Define the term 'expected life event'.
                                    (2 marks)

Expected life events 2

Expected life events can have positive and negative effects on a person's growth and development.

Positive and negative effects

Expected life event	Positive effects on development		Negative effects on development	
Starting nursery, school, college or university	✓	• Build new friendships • Learn and develop new skills • Improved self-esteem	✗	• Anxiety about new routines and meeting new people • Young children may feel insecure when leaving their parents for the first time
Getting a new job	✓	• Develop independence • Improve self-image and self-esteem • Build new relationships • Learn new skills (for example, creative thinking, problem solving)	✗	• Stress and anxiety
Living with a partner/getting married/entering a civil partnership	✓	• Feel secure and content • Develop intimate relationships	✗	• Loss of independence • Have to share
Moving house or area	✓	• Excited by a new challenge • Develop new friendships/relationships	✗	• Loss of friends • Anxiety and stress of moving • May feel isolated
Becoming a parent	✓	• Feel content • Improved emotional wellbeing • Develop strong attachments	✗	• Worry about responsibility • Feel tired • Loss of independence
Retirement	✓	• Reduced stress • Socialise more with family and friends	✗	• Loss of relationships • May have negative self-image • May lose mobility/fitness

Worked example

Krysta, aged 62, lives with her husband Stefan, aged 65. Krysta recently retired from her job. Stefan retired last year. They have three children and two grandchildren, all of whom live nearby.

Explain **one** possible positive and **one** possible negative effect of Krysta's life events on her development.   **(4 marks)**

Positive: Krysta is likely to feel more contented as she has more time to spend with her family.

Negative: She may lose formal relationships as she is no longer working.

Read the question carefully. You need to think about **both** positive and negative effects.

Now try this

Drew has just left university with a good degree. He has been offered a job at a local IT company.

Give **two** possible reasons why Drew has a positive self-image.   **(2 marks)**

Unexpected life events 1

Unexpected life events are those that happen during the course of life and that cannot be predicted.

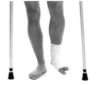

Death of someone close to you   Accident/injury

Ill health ——— **Unexpected life events** ——— Imprisonment

Promotion   Redundancy

Dropping out of education

> **Key term**
> REDUNDANCY: when a company no longer needs a particular job so they let the employee go

Worked example

Identify the correct types of life event listed below.
Draw lines to match each event to the correct type.   **(4 marks)**

Life event   **Type of event**

Road accident

                              Expected life event

Leaving school

Imprisonment

                              Unexpected life event

Retirement

> If you have to **match** lines in the exam, draw a neat pencil line using a ruler. If you need to change your answer, it's better to put a line through the original line rather than use an eraser. This makes it clearer which line shows your final answer.

Now try this

Darren is 29 years old. He shares a flat with his wife Leanne. Darren has worked as a manager in a sports shop since he left college, but last month he was made redundant. Leanne has been ill with depression since her mum died last year.

Give **one** example of an unexpected life event for Darren and **one** example for Leanne.

(2 marks)

> Read the case study carefully, as Darren and Leanne have experienced both **expected** and **unexpected** life events.

Unexpected life events 2

Unexpected life events can have positive or negative effects. Here are some examples.

Unexpected life event	Possible effects
Accidents, injury or ill health	• Loss of mobility • Depression • Restriction in social activities • A lack of interest in appearance
Death of a partner, relative or friend	• A feeling of loss and grief • Low self-confidence • Loss of friends • Unable to cope/function at work
Exclusion/dropping out of education	• Low self-esteem • Loss of friends • Restriction in social activities
Imprisonment	• Depression • Loss of social contact • Low self-esteem • Loss of independence
Promotion	• Improved self-esteem • Positive self-image • More independence
Redundancy	• Low self-esteem • Stress • Fewer opportunities for learning and developing skills • Fewer opportunities to interact/develop new relationships (for example, with colleagues) • Opportunities to train for a new job

Family and friends

Unexpected life events can affect not only an individual but also their family and friends. For example:

• relationships – damage to relationships between partners and other family members

• emotional stress on partners, family and friends – people need physical and emotional support from them

• distress – family and friends may find it hard to accept the new situation.

Layla has one child, Hasim, aged 3. She has recently been promoted at work. The new job requires her to work longer hours.

Give **two** possible effects of Layla's promotion at work on Hasim's development. **(2 marks)**

1 Hasim may not bond as well with his mother.

2 Hasim may feel insecure and anxious.

For questions that ask you to **give** possible effects, it is enough just to state the effects, without extending the answer to give reasons!

'Explain' questions require you to develop your answer. In your answer to this question, identify **two** effects and then extend your sentence to give the reason for each.

Craig lives with his partner Eva. He was recently caught stealing a car and has been given a 12-month prison sentence.

Explain **two** ways in which going to prison may affect Craig's emotional and social development. **(4 marks)**

Types of support

People may need SUPPORT when they experience expected and/or unexpected life events.

FORMAL – physical or emotional support from trained professionals (for example, doctors, care workers)

EMOTIONAL – support for coping with feelings (for example, counselling)

Types of support

PHYSICAL – support for day-to-day care needs (for example, help with mobility or shopping)

INFORMAL – unpaid physical or emotional support from family and friends

Worked example

Define the terms 'formal' support and 'informal' support. **(2 marks)**

Formal support is support given by trained healthcare professionals who are paid to provide it.

Informal support is unpaid support provided by family and friends.

Informal support is classed as unpaid support. However, some families may still receive an allowance to help them to stay at home to provide support.

Helping someone with mobility difficulties to shop is an example of informal support.

Now try this

1 Define the terms 'physical support' and 'emotional support'. **(2 marks)**

Roger is 54 years old. He lives with his partner, Jakob. Roger no longer works as he has muscular dystrophy, which has caused muscle loss and weakness. He now has to use a wheelchair.

2 Give **one** example of physical support and **one** example of emotional support that Roger may need. **(2 marks)**

Can you identify whether your examples are **formal** or **informal** types of support? For instance, Roger may receive formal physical support from a professional, or informal physical support from Jakob.

Managing change 1

FORMAL and INFORMAL support can help with dealing with life events in a number of ways.

Formal support

Formal support may be given by different professionals, such as district nurses, social care workers, counsellors and physiotherapists.

Providing for health needs such as changing dressings or prescribing medication

Advising and helping with exercise to improve mobility

Referring people to other services that can help

Managing expectations about health and welfare

Support provided by professional carers

Counselling to give people the opportunity to talk about their worries

Liaising with other professionals to provide care

Advising individuals and their family about a health or social problem and ways to improve own health and welfare

Informal support

Informal support may be given by family and/or friends.

Support to maintain independence

Help with washing and dressing

Support provided by family and friends

Reassurance

Help with day-to-day tasks, such as shopping and cleaning

Support with coming to terms with changes in health or circumstances

Help in coping with change

Worked example

Mary is 77 years old and lives with her adult daughter, Claire. Mary recently had a fall and broke her hip. This has upset her, as she has always been very active. Mary has now been discharged from hospital. She is happy to be at home, but is still experiencing pain. She is being visited by the district nurse.

Identify **one** type of support that Mary may need from the district nurse and **one** type of support she may need from Claire.   **(2 marks)**

1 Mary may need the district nurse to administer medication for the pain.

2 Mary may need Claire to help her come to terms with her accident.

When answering questions about the **types** of support that an individual might need, read the information about the person carefully. It will give you clues to the type of support needed.

To answer this question, refer back to the case study in the worked example.

Now try this

Give **one** possible effect of Mary being supported in her own home on her emotional development and **one** possible effect on her social development.   **(2 marks)**

Managing change 2

There are different types of voluntary organisation that offer support to people who are affected by life events. These organisations are non-profit making.

VOLUNTARY ORGANISATIONS (national or local)
- Support people with particular needs, for example:
  - health needs, such as diabetes or dementia
  - welfare needs, such as bereavement
- Provide specialist information and advice
- May work alongside professionals offering formal support

Types of voluntary support

COMMUNITY GROUPS
- Based in the local area
- Understand the needs of local people
- Include SELF-HELP GROUPS
- Offer a range of support (for example, providing transport for people who can't drive, food banks for low waged/unemployed)

RELIGIOUS GROUPS
- Linked to a particular faith
- Provide support and promote the health and welfare of people from particular religious groups
- Support and advice is based on religious beliefs/morals

Key term

SELF-HELP GROUPS: groups that come together to give each other support

Worked example

Nazia is 67 years old. She is a Muslim. Since the death of her husband last year, she has lived alone. She is still finding it difficult to cope with the bereavement.

Explain **two** ways in which support from a local religious group may help Nazia to manage the change in her life caused by bereavement.

(4 marks)

Nazia may feel more secure when receiving support from an organisation based on her own faith, because they hold the same religious beliefs and values as her and will therefore be more understanding. For example, they will know that, as a Muslim woman, she may prefer the support to be given by another woman. By understanding her faith and beliefs, they will be more likely to be able to help her come to terms with her feelings.

Food banks help those on low wages or who are unemployed.

This answer takes into account **both** religion and culture.

Now try this

Give **two** examples of the type of support that people may need from a voluntary organisation.

(2 marks)

Exam skills 1

You will have one hour to complete all the questions in your test paper. The paper is worth 50 marks. It is divided into two main sections, which are broken down into a number of questions. Each question relates to a case study.

What is a case study?

A case study gives you information about a family, a group of people or an individual. It may include information such as ages, details of relationships, lifestyle choices and any events that have happened to them.

It will help you if you try to imagine the people described in each case study.

Why are case studies used?

Case studies show that you can apply your knowledge and understanding of the content to real-life situations. For example, in Unit I, you will apply knowledge about:

- different life stages
- key aspects of human growth and development
- factors that affect human growth and development
- life events that can affect human growth and development
- types of support available to help people to manage change caused by life events.

Case study example

The following information is about the Taylor family.

Martin is 53 years old. His partner Penny is 42 years old. They have two children: Todd is 8 years old and Claire is 15 years old.

Penny works full-time as a secretary. Martin has just been made redundant from his job as a call centre manager.

Penny's mum, Sarah, is 65 years old and lives close by. She has recently retired from her job as an accountant.

This case study gives you the age of each person in the family. Knowing their age tells you the **life stage** that each person has reached. For example, Todd is in the early childhood life stage.

This tells you that Martin has experienced an **unexpected life event**. You might be asked how this may affect his development.

This tells you about Penny's mum, Sarah. You might be asked how **retirement** may affect her intellectual development.

Preparation

It is really important that you prepare well for your test. Give yourself plenty of time.

Pace yourself

- Think about how you learn best – create materials that suit you.
- Start revision with plenty of time – plan it out.
- Try and avoid distractions – find somewhere suitable to work.

Hints and tips

- You can do the questions in any order – if you're struggling, leave one and carry on.
- You do NOT lose marks for a wrong answer, so your best guess is better than a blank space.
- Use the marks given to guide you on your answer.

Exam skills 2

The exam paper contains different TYPES OF QUESTION. Understanding the types of questions will help you to answer them more easily and organise your time more efficiently.

Types of question

Objective questions	Require a short answer to show your knowledge
Short-answer questions	Require more information to show that you understand 'how' or 'why'
Extended questions	Require more detail to show that you understand the relationships between different aspects of a topic

Command words

It is important that you understand COMMAND WORDS in questions, as they tell you how much information you need to give to answer the question fully. See OBJECTIVE QUESTIONS below and the two following pages for information on command words for different types of question.

Number of marks and time

At the end of each question, you will be given the marks available in brackets. This helps you understand how much information you need to give in your answer.

It is important that you spend the right amount of time on each type of question so you do not run out of time.

Objective questions

In objective questions, you will come across command words such as IDENTIFY, GIVE, STATE, DEFINE and OUTLINE. For questions that use these words you need to give a brief, precise response without going into detail.

Types of objective question

Some objective questions may require you to:
• draw a line from information leading to the correct answer
• put a cross by the correct answer.

Example of an objective question

'Define' is asking you to give the meaning of a word or an idea.

Read these types of question very carefully to ensure that you give the correct number of examples. The number required is always given in bold.

Tyronne is 16 years old. He is experiencing puberty and is struggling with his self-image. He has just left school and is about to start a college course in business studies.

1 Identify Tyronne's life stage. **(1 mark)**

2 Define the term 'self-image'. **(1 mark)**

3 Give **two** examples of the **social** skills that Tyronne is developing at his life stage. **(2 marks)**

Leaving school will be an expected life event for Tyronne.

4 Outline the difference between expected and unexpected life events. **(2 marks)**

At the end of the question you will see the number of marks in brackets.

This is an objective question. The following brief response would be sufficient: 'Tyronne is in the adolescent life stage.'

'Outline' only needs a brief description.

Exam skills 3

In SHORT ANSWER QUESTIONS, you need to develop your answers to gain full marks. There will also be one EXTENDED ANSWER QUESTION on your exam paper. This will be worth eight marks.

Answering short answer questions

- Unlike with objective questions, it isn't enough just to state or list information.
- When asked to EXPLAIN, you need to justify what you are saying or give reasons.
- Using the words BECAUSE or THEREFORE in your sentence will make sure that you develop your answer.
- Refer directly to the information given in a case study, such as a person's life stage factors that may affect their development or a life event.
- Write the correct number of sentences. For example, if the question reads 'Explain **two** effects on development', you must write TWO sentences.

In the test, underline the key words in the question. This will help you to answer the question fully and gain all the marks available.

In this example, two sentences are needed: one about the **positive** effect of starting nursery and one about the **negative** effect of starting nursery. Both sentences should relate to emotional development.

Worked example

Talicia is 2 years old. She will be starting nursery next month when her mum returns to work.

Explain **one** possible **positive** and **one** possible **negative** effect of starting nursery on Talicia's emotional development.   **(4 marks)**

Positive: Talicia will be cared for by someone else so will learn how to build new attachments/relationships.

Negative: Talicia will have formed strong attachments with her mother and may become anxious because she misses her when at nursery.

Extended answer question

In an extended answer question, you will need to write at length about, for example:
- a person's stage of growth and development
- factors that affect them
- life events
- how a person may be supported.

Command words in extended answer questions

ASSESS – To do this, you must look at the factors or events that are relevant to the individual(s) or situation and consider how they relate to each other.

EVALUATE – To do this, you must review the information given from different points of view and form a conclusion.

Steps to success with extended answer questions

1 Read the case study and question carefully.

2 Read it through again and underline or highlight each key word.

3 Break the topic down into parts to make sure that you include all relevant points.

4 Write a brief plan of what you want to include before you start.

Answer space

For each type of question (objective, short answer and extended), use the space available to write your answer. The amount of space will give you an idea of how much information is needed.

Exam skills 4

It is important to follow the steps to success given on the previous page if you want to get the maximum marks available in extended answer questions. Below is an example of an extended answer question, along with a suggested answer.

The learner has underlined the key pieces of information to help them to plan the answer. They have underlined other family members and their ages as well as the information about Adil. This is important, because the impact of the life event will be felt by them too. The age of each family member may also be relevant to the type of support they may be able to give.

Worked example

Adil is aged 54 and he is married to Meena, who is 44 years old. Adil worked full time until recently, when he had a serious accident at work. Adil needed an operation on his back. He is now home from the hospital, but he is still in pain and unable to walk. Adil and Meena have a daughter Naara, aged 22, who lives close by.

Other key pieces of information are that this was a serious accident, that it is still causing pain for Adil and that he is unable to walk. This indicates the types of support he will need.

Assess the support that Adil and his family might need to manage the recent unexpected life event.   **(8 marks)**

It is always advisable to underline the command word – in this question, it is **assess**. This indicates the detail you must provide. This learner has also underlined the words 'support' and 'his family', which will help to remind the learner to include information on the support needed by Adil **and** his wife and daughter.

Adil may need formal support from a district nurse to give him medication for the pain. The nurse may need to coordinate other formal services, such as physiotherapy, to help to improve Adil's mobility and give advice to Meena.

The learner has planned the answer well to ensure that there is an equal balance between the four key types of support: formal, informal, physical and emotional.

Adil may need formal support from a counsellor to help him, Meena and Naara to come to terms with their feelings, such as depression and anxiety, after the accident.

Adil may need informal support from Meena to do everyday physical tasks, such as washing and dressing. He may need Meena to listen to him and give him reassurance.

The learner shows that they have read the detail about the accident and refers to this. For instance, they note that Adil is unable to walk, so his mobility is affected, and that Naara lives close by, so is able to give support to both Adil and Meena.

Naara, who lives nearby, may need to give support to both Adil, her father, and Meena, her mother, by preparing food and helping her father with tasks when her mother is at work. Naara may also support Meena by listening to her mother's worries about Adil's health.

The learner also understand how Meena and Naara's lives and feelings may have been affected by the accident.

Defining health and wellbeing

It is important that you know and understand the correct definitions of health and wellbeing.

World Health Organization

The World Health Organization (WHO) defines health as 'a complete state of physical, mental and social wellbeing, and not merely the absence of disease or infirmity' (Source: WHO, 1948).

This is a holistic definition, which means it is to do with you as a whole person.

There are four needs that affect health and wellbeing:

1 PHYSICAL NEEDS
2 INTELLECTUAL NEEDS
3 EMOTIONAL NEEDS
4 SOCIAL NEEDS

If you take the first letter of each type of need, they spell PIES.

There is more about these four needs on the next two pages.

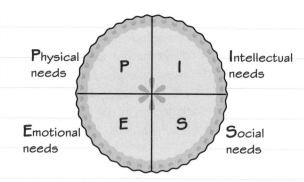

Key terms

PHYSICAL NEEDS: these relate to the health of your body

INTELLECTUAL NEEDS: these relate to your brain and your ability to think and understand

EMOTIONAL NEEDS: these relate to your feelings

SOCIAL NEEDS: these relate to your relationships with others

Worked example

Give **two** needs that are important to health and wellbeing.   **(2 marks)**

1 Physical needs

2 Emotional needs

The question asks for two needs. Make sure you pick two **different** needs rather than naming one and defining it, for example:

✓ Physical needs
✗ To do with the body

They are to do with same thing and would not be a good answer.

Now try this

Compare the WHO definition with the four types of needs if you don't know the answer to this.

1 Which **two** types of needs are mental wellbeing associated with?   **(2 marks)**

2 Explain why the definition of health and wellbeing is described as holistic.   **(1 mark)**

Physical and intellectual factors

Physical needs relate to keeping the body healthy and intellectual needs relate to keeping the brain active.

Meeting physical needs

Reduced chance of illness

Healthy body systems

Effects of meeting physical needs

Healthy weight maintenance

Higher energy levels

Improved fitness

Basic needs

Everybody has the same basic needs for survival. These are:
- food
- water
- shelter
- warmth
- clothing
- rest
- exercise
- good personal hygiene.

Meeting intellectual needs

Our brains need MENTAL STIMULATION to meet our intellectual needs and prevent us from being bored. Mental stimulation keeps us interested and motivated so we can take advantage of learning opportunities.

You need to be able to:
- concentrate so you can absorb facts, the opinions of others or instructions, and gain the knowledge, understanding and skills you need to succeed in life
- think clearly to be able to solve problems
- develop the ability to learn throughout life, to keep your brain active and healthy.

Improved concentration

Effects of meeting intellectual needs

The ability to learn

Clearer thinking

Balance is important

These basic needs have to be balanced to get the best effects. For example, eating too little or too much food can result in being underweight or obese.

Worked example

Which **two** of the following are physical effects of taking the correct amount of exercise?   **(2 marks)**

A ✓ Healthy body systems
B ☐ Improved concentration
C ✓ Improved fitness
D ☐ Good mental health
E ☐ Improved self-esteem

Make sure you read the question carefully. **Physical** means to do with our bodies.

Now try this

Concentration is an important part of meeting our intellectual needs.
Give **two** reasons why it is important to be able to concentrate.   **(2 marks)**

Emotional and social effects

Emotional needs relate to feelings. Social needs relate to relationships.

Emotional needs

Our basic emotional needs are to feel:
- loved
- wanted
- respected
- supported
- secure
- needed.

If these needs are met, you will feel the benefits shown in the diagram below.

> ### Key terms
> SELF-ESTEEM: how much you value yourself
> SELF-IMAGE: the mental image you have of yourself

Meeting emotional needs

It is important that emotional needs are met to help cope with different situations throughout life.

Greater levels of happiness · Improved mood · Improved self-confidence · Good mental health · **Effects of meeting emotional needs** · Improved self-esteem · Reduced stress · Positive self-image · Improved motivational levels · Increased emotional resilience · Developing and maintaining close intimate and sexual relationships

Social needs

It is very important to be able to develop and enjoy good relationships and friendships, and have a good social life. In order to do this, you need:
- opportunities to mix with others
- an appropriate environment in which to mix with others – to ensure you are comfortable, relaxed and feel safe
- access to leisure facilities
- access to leisure activities.

Meeting social needs

Improved quality of social life · Closer friendships · **Effects of meeting social needs** · Extended patterns of social relationships

Which **one** of the following is a reason why it is important that our emotional needs are met?   **(1 mark)**

A ☐ To keep our brains active   B ☐ To allow us to express our feelings

C ☐ To keep our bodies working   D ☑ So that we can develop good relationships and friendships

> Make sure you only tick **one** box. If you change your mind about your answer put a line through the box you have ticked.

Explain why it is necessary to have opportunities to mix with others and somewhere appropriate to do this.

(2 marks)

Physical effects of an unhealthy lifestyle

The three main physical effects of an unhealthy lifestyle are diseases and illness, weight gain or loss and a high or low body fat composition. These can lead to short- and long-term health problems.

 Diseases and illnesses

Conditions that can be caused by an unhealthy lifestyle (these can be controlled)	Inherited genetic conditions (we have no control over these)
• Cancers – due to obesity, excessive alcohol, smoking • Liver disease – due to excessive alcohol • Heart disease – due to obesity and stress • Sexually transmitted infections (STIs) – due to unprotected sex	• Cystic fibrosis • Down's syndrome • Muscular dystrophy • Haemophilia • Sickle cell disease

 Weight gain or loss

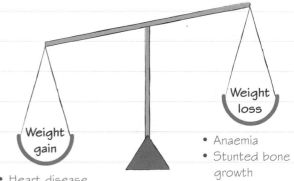

Weight gain
• Heart disease
• Type 2 diabetes
• Cancers
• High blood pressure

Weight loss
• Anaemia
• Stunted bone growth

 Body fat composition

This is the percentage of body fat that a person has.

RIGHT AMOUNT OF BODY FAT
✓ • Body temperature regulated
• Right amount of energy stored
• Organs and tissues cushioned and insulated

TOO LITTLE BODY FAT
✗ • Brittle bones
• Body temperature too cold
• Fertility problems

TOO MUCH BODY FAT
✗ • Obesity
• Body temperature too hot
• Increased risk of many diseases

An unhealthy lifestyle can cause short- and long-term effects. For example, stress can cause many effects, but an example of a short-term one is pains in the stomach, and a long-term one is high blood pressure.

Worked example

Leah is 15 years old and spends her lunch money on junk food. Name **two** physical effects this may have on her. **(2 marks)**

1 Weight gain
2 Too much sugar may lead to tooth decay

 The number of marks tells you how many different reasons are needed.

Now try this

Explain **one** reason why it is important to have a healthy body fat composition. **(2 marks)**

43

Intellectual effects of an unhealthy lifestyle

The three main intellectual effects of an unhealthy lifestyle are reduced potential success in education, a negative impact on long-term career prospects and an inability to think clearly.

 Reduced educational success

An unhealthy lifestyle can result in:

- being ill more often and so poor attendance at school
- slower brain development due to a poor diet.

Vitamins and minerals

- Vitamin B6 is needed for brain development.
- Iron is needed for correct functioning of the brain.
- Other vitamins (B6, B12, E), minerals (magnesium) and folic acid are also needed.

 Poor long-term career prospects

An unhealthy lifestyle leading to reduced educational success could result in poor long-term career prospects.

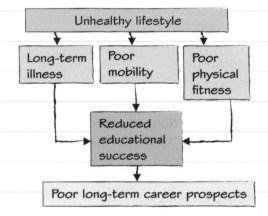

 Inability to think clearly

The following factors could affect your ability to think clearly.

The effects of drug abuse — **Inability to think clearly** — The effects of alcohol

Hunger — Feeling ill

Nowhere quiet to work/study

Look at the image by this question to find your answers.

Now try this

Worked example

Explain how poor physical fitness caused by an unhealthy lifestyle might affect your educational success and long-term career prospects. **(2 marks)**

1 You may be ill more often so have poor attendance at school, leading to few qualifications or poor qualification results.

2 You may have limited mobility, which reduces the number of jobs at which you can be successful.

Identify **two** factors that are preventing this learner from thinking clearly. **(2 marks)**

Emotional effects of an unhealthy lifestyle

You need to know some of the ways in which an unhealthy lifestyle can affect an individual's emotional wellbeing.

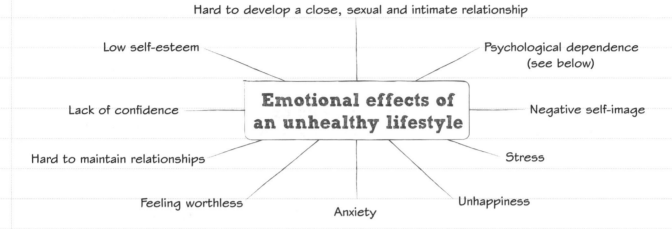

Key terms

PSYCHOLOGICAL DEPENDENCE: an emotional need for a substance or activity that is not needed physically. It results in a craving to take a substance into your body (for example, cigarettes or drugs) or take part in a certain activity (for example, gambling). Other examples are shown to the right.

CLOSE SEXUAL AND INTIMATE RELATIONSHIP: a happy, successful physical relationship that helps you meet your basic needs – PIES (see page 40 to remind yourself of this)

SELF-IMAGE and SELF-ESTEEM: see page 42 for an explanation of the difference

Examples of psychological dependencies

- ⊗ Smoking
- ⊗ Self-harming
- ⊗ Gambling
- ⊗ Shopping
- ⊗ Taking drugs
- ⊗ Drinking alcohol
- ⊗ Eating
- ⊗ Sniffing solvents

Worked example

Ashiq is 19 years old and spends all his time and money gambling online.

Identify **two** likely emotional effects of this unhealthy lifestyle. **(2 marks)**

1 Stress

2 Difficulties starting and keeping close relationships

For example, if the psychological dependence were food, think about the likely effects of eating too much on a person's confidence and body image.

Now try this

Describe how a psychological dependence could lead to problems in developing a close, sexual and intimate relationship. **(4 marks)**

45

Social effects of an unhealthy lifestyle

You need to know some of the ways that an unhealthy lifestyle can affect an individual's social wellbeing.

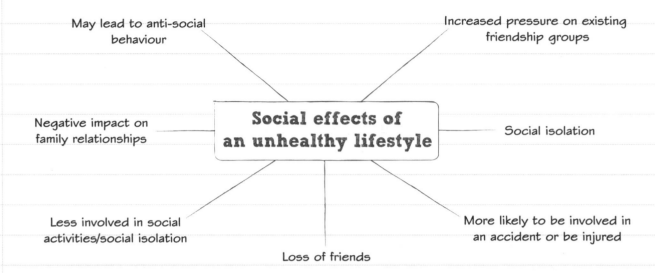

Social effect	Example
Loss of friends	Individuals may steal from friends to buy drugs or alcohol.
Increased pressure on existing friendship groups	Individuals may try to persuade their friends to drink or take drugs.
Negative impact on family relationships	Individuals may fall out with family members who do not approve of their lifestyle choices.
Less involved in social activities/social isolation	Individuals may not be invited to join in if they behave aggressively, as a result of alcohol or drugs, or may lack the self-esteem to join in.
More likely to be involved in an accident/get injured in a fight/be involved in anti-social behaviour	Individuals who are dependent on substances may be more likely to get injured or engage in anti-social behavioiur under the influence.

Worked example

Zoltán is 29 years old and is a drug addict. State **three** possible social effects of his unhealthy lifestyle.   **(3 marks)**

1 Loss of friends

2 Social isolation

3 Increased risk of injury

Pay attention to the command word in a question as it will guide you on how much you should write.

Now try this

State **three** ways in which Zoltán's dependency on drugs might have a negative impact on his family relationships.   **(3 marks)**

Diet and nutrition

A balanced diet has the right proportion of nutrients to keep your mind and body healthy.

Nutrients needed	Purpose	Examples
Fats (saturated and unsaturated)	Source of energy	Saturated: butter, meat fat Unsaturated: vegetable oil
Carbohydrates (sugars and starches)	Source of energy	Sugars: sweets, cakes Starches: pasta, potatoes
Proteins	Growth and repair of cells and tissues	Meat, fish, cheese, eggs, nuts, seeds
Vitamins	Help the body function properly – for example: • A – healthy skin • B – energy and healthy brain • C – healthy immune system • D – healthy teeth/bones	Dairy products, fruit, vegetables
Minerals	Help with bones, teeth, blood, skin, hair and nerve function – for example: • calcium – for strong bones • iron – for haemoglobin for transporting oxygen and CO_2 around the body)	Dairy products, fruit, vegetables, fish

The body also needs fibre; which helps digestion and excretion and is found in beans and cereals, and water; an essential part of all body cells and that helps many chemical reactions in the body.

Recommended daily intake

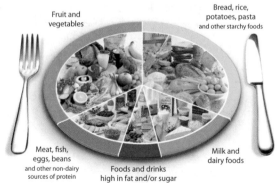

The eatwell plate

Use the eatwell plate to help you get the balance right. It shows how much of what you eat should come from each food group.

Fruit and vegetables

Bread, rice, potatoes, pasta and other starchy foods

Meat, fish, eggs, beans and other non-dairy sources of protein

Foods and drinks high in fat and/or sugar

Milk and dairy foods

© Crown copyright 2013

Public Health England in association with the Welsh Government, the Scottish Government and the Food Standards Agency in Northern Ireland

An unbalanced diet

Eating too much or too little can lead to:

- ⊗ obesity
- ⊗ diabetes
- ⊗ coronary heart disease/heart failure
- ⊗ high blood pressure
- ⊗ cancers
- ⊗ strokes
- ⊗ excessive weight loss/anorexia.

Worked example

Identify **two** possible physical effects of eating too much.   **(2 marks)**

A ☐ Anorexia   B ☐ Scurvy

C ☑ Obesity   D ☑ High blood pressure

E ☐ Weight loss

Think about how food helps the body to function.

Now try this

Explain **one** reason why eating too little could lead to poor health.   **(2 marks)**

Exercise

Exercise is another factor in a healthy or unhealthy lifestyle.

Physical benefits of exercise

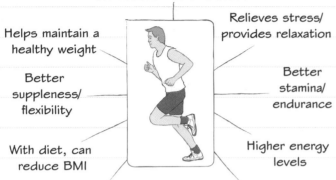

Can reduce risk of disease

Relieves stress/ provides relaxation

Helps maintain a healthy weight

Better stamina/ endurance

Better suppleness/ flexibility

With diet, can reduce BMI

Higher energy levels

Better strength

Aids weight loss

Frequency and level

- Take some exercise every day.
- Take AEROBIC CARDIOVASCULAR EXERCISE 3–5 times a week for at least 20 minutes each time.
- The level of exercise should be appropriate to your stage in life.

Key term

AEROBIC CARDIOVASCULAR EXERCISE: includes running, cycling and swimming, and raises the heart rate for a period of time

Body mass index

Exercise and diet can help maintain a healthy weight and healthy BMI (BODY MASS INDEX). BMI is a measure of the amount of fat in your body based on your weight and height.

To work out a person's BMI you need the following formula:

$$BMI = \frac{Weight\ in\ kg}{(Height\ in\ m)^2}$$

Interpreting BMI

Once you have calculated a person's BMI you can use the range in the table below to determine their BMI category.

BMI range	BMI category
<19	Underweight
20–25	Desirable
25–30	Overweight
31+	Obese

A **health improvement plan** may be based on reducing a person's BMI. BMI is used by medical professionals as an important indicator of health. A person who is obese may be asked to lose weight before being allowed to have a non-urgent operation.

Understanding BMI

If your BMI is in the normal range, you are more likely to live longer.

BEWARE: BMI only takes weight and height into account, but ignores the distribution of muscle and bone mass. So a muscular person may have a high BMI even if they are fit and healthy.

Worked example

Duane is 1.75 m tall and weighs 73 kg.

Calculate his BMI to one decimal place. **(2 marks)**

$$BMI = \frac{Weight\ in\ kg}{(Height\ in\ m)^2} = \frac{73}{1.75^2} = \frac{73}{3.06}$$

BMI = 23.8 kg/m²

Always show your workings.

Now try this

Shara is 1.6 m tall and weighs 70 kg.

(a) Calculate her BMI to one decimal place.
    (2 marks)

(b) Using the table above, which BMI category is Shara in? **(1 mark)**

BMI ranges and meanings vary. Always use the chart you are given.

Home environment

The environment in which you live affects your lifestyle, as you spend a lot of time there. The physical effects of an unhealthy home environment are an increased chance of illness, diseases and health problems, or worsening of existing health conditions, such as asthma.

The condition and location of our home environment

May be small, cramped, cluttered

May be noisier, for example noisy neighbours causing sleeplessness

More likely to have accidents in the home

Poorer living conditions

Less likely to have outdoor space for children to play in

May be damp, cold and dirty so more prone to illness

More conflict, for example due to stress, cramped conditions

Often found in urban areas, which may be affected by pollution

More likely to be quiet/peaceful, resulting in better sleep

Likely to be more spacious

Likely to have outdoor space for children to play in

Better living conditions

A better environment is more likely to make people happier and less likely to make them ill

Access to services may be more difficult in rural/isolated areas

Personal space

If you share a room, you may have less:

- ☒ privacy
- ☒ space for your belongings
- ☒ space to do your schoolwork
- ☒ space for hobbies.

Due to less personal space, you may be:

- ☒ more disorganised
- ☒ less motivated
- ☒ unable to concentrate.

The influence of partners and family

Those you live with influence:

- what you eat
- how you dress
- your moods and behaviour
- your motivation
- your behaviour and habits, for example:
  - whether you exercise
  - whether you smoke or take substances
  - your attitude to safe sex
  - your personal hygiene.

Worked example

Explain **two** ways that poor living conditions can lead to an unhealthy lifestyle.   **(2 marks)**

1 May not get enough sleep if the conditions are cold, damp or overcrowded. As a result they are more likely to be ill.

2 May relieve boredom by smoking or taking drugs, because others living with or near them do the same.

Think about PIES (page 40) when answering this question.

Now try this

Describe **two** ways in which better living conditions can improve a person's health and wellbeing.   **(4 marks)**

Had a look ☐ Nearly there ☐ Nailed it! ☐

Work environment

You will spend a large proportion of your adult life at work, and your work environment can have a huge impact on your health and wellbeing.

Work-related factors

The following work-related factors may affect your health and wellbeing.

Factor	Advantages	Disadvantages
Type of work (manual/ non-manual)	✓ • Manual work is physically hard, so can improve physical fitness. • It is usually less stressful. • You are less likely to be involved in an accident or sustain an injury in non-manual work.	✗ • Manual work is more likely to involve accidents and injuries. • Non-manual work is sedentary so less physically active. • It may also be more stressful. • Sitting at a computer may cause problems with eyesight and posture.
Job satisfaction	✓ • Varied work is more enjoyable.	✗ • Routine work can be dissatisfying.
Mental stimulation	✓ • A varied, stimulating job gives you opportunities to learn.	✗ • Routine jobs may be boring.
Career success	✓ • Success and career progression can improve self-esteem and confidence.	✗ • Jobs with more responsibility can be more stressful.
Support from colleagues, or conflict	✓ • You can develop life-long friendships and a good social life with colleagues.	✗ • Poor working relationships (for example, with your employer) can cause stress and conflict.
Work/life balance	✓ • High-powered jobs usually pay good salaries.	✗ • A well-paid job may: ◦ be demanding ◦ require long hours ◦ give you less time outside work.

Work/life balance

It is important to work to live, not live to work.

POOR WORK/LIFE BALANCE

Work   Life: unhappy as no time for self/family

GOOD WORK/LIFE BALANCE

Work   Life: happy as time for self/family

Worked example

Which **two** of the following are ways in which a successful, demanding job might contribute to an unhealthy lifestyle?   **(2 marks)**

A ☐ It can lead to a lack of confidence
B ☑ It can be stressful
C ☑ Longer hours and less time at home may result in poor eating habits or skipping meals
D ☐ It is poorly paid
E ☐ It can lead to low self-esteem

Now try this

Identify **two** ways in which a non-manual job might contribute to an unhealthy lifestyle.   **(2 marks)**

Alcohol consumption

Levels of alcohol consumption can have an effect on health and wellbeing.

This table shows the maximum regular consumption levels for men and women.

	Units (day)	Units (week)	Alcohol-free days per week
Men	3–4	21	At least 2
Women	2–3	14	At least 2

Pregnant women

Pregnant women are advised not to drink.

How many units of alcohol?

2	1.5	1.5	1	10
Pint of beer/lager /cider	Alcopop or can of lager	Glass of wine (125 ml)	Single measure of spirits	Bottle of wine

Binge drinking

This is drinking heavily in a short space of time, to feel the effects of alcohol more. Binge drinking is drinking more than double the daily recommended units in one session.

The main PHYSICAL EFFECTS are:
• vomiting
• loss of sensory perception
• blackouts.

Alcohol dependence

This is a physical and mental need to drink alcohol and the inability to stop. It is a CHRONIC and PROGRESSIVE disease.
Alcohol dependence can:
☒ result in cravings for alcohol
☒ cause withdrawal symptoms if you stop
☒ have physical, social and emotional effects
☒ have long-term health risks
☒ result in premature death.

Underage drinking

In the UK, you must be:
• 18 years old to buy alcohol
• 16 years old and accompanied by an adult to drink alcohol with a meal in a licensed public place.

How it happens

UNDERAGE DRINKING happens as a result of:
☒ peer pressure
☒ low prices
☒ alcohol being readily available
☒ parents or older friends buying it.

Key terms

CHRONIC: long-term
PROGRESSIVE: effects become more severe over time

Worked example

Which of the following is the definition of 'binge drinking'? **(1 mark)**

A ☐ Drinking a small amount in a short space of time

B ☐ Drinking a large amount over a long period of time

C ☐ Drinking three times the daily unit guidelines in one session

D ☑ Drinking double the daily unit guidelines in one session

Now try this

Laura regularly drinks too much. She has tried to stop but can't.

Explain **two** ways in which alcohol dependence could affect Laura's physical health and emotional wellbeing in the long term. **(4 marks)**

This question is about long-term effects, so do not include short-term effects.

Effects of alcohol

When drunk in moderation, ALCOHOL may have HEALTH BENEFITS, but it can cause serious RISKS to your health and wellbeing if drunk in excess.

Possible physical effects

- ✗ Long-term and short-term health risks
- ✗ Accidents or injuries resulting from impaired judgement
- ✗ Unsafe sexual practice resulting from impaired judgement
- ✓ Health benefits (see below)

Possible emotional, social and intellectual effects

- ✗ Alcohol dependence (or alcoholism) – more information can be found on page 51
- ✗ Mental health/social issues such as:
  - anxiety
  - depression
  - irritability
  - relationship problems

Health benefits

If an adult drinks alcohol in small quantities (for example, a glass of red wine a day up to five days a week), this can have some benefits.

Can decrease risk of dementia

Can help prevent colds

Small quantities of alcohol

May reduce risk of gallstones

May lower risk of diabetes

Can lower risk of cardiovascular disease

Health risks

If an adult regularly drinks over the guideline amounts of alcohol there can be health risks.

Infertility/impotence

Stomach/intestinal ulcers

Heart disease

Osteoporosis

Excessive alcohol consumption

Cancer

Weight gain

Brain damage, addiction, stroke

Liver disease/ liver failure

Mental health issues

Worked example

Identify **two** ways in which drinking alcohol in moderation can be beneficial. **(2 marks)**

1 Alcohol may lower the risk of cardiovascular disease.

2 Alcohol may decrease the risk of dementia.

Now try this

Which of these is **not** a health risk associated with excessive alcohol consumption? **(1 mark)**

A ☐ Liver disease

B ☐ Lung cancer

C ☐ Weight gain

D ☐ Mental health issues

Smoking

Smoking is bad for your health and can cause premature death.

Reasons people smoke

- Peer pressure – most smokers start as teenagers, to be like their friends, to try to look older, to experiment and to rebel
- As a reward – for example, when they have completed a task at work
- To relieve stress
- To beat other addictions, such as drugs or alcohol
- To feel relaxed
- To help them cope with a hard time
- To control weight
- For pleasure

How quantity affects health

The more cigarettes smoked, the greater the damage caused. The damage is even greater if the cigarettes have no filters.

Smoking ban

In the UK, smoking is now banned in all public places, including indoor workplaces, public transport and most work vehicles and company cars.

How addiction happens

- Nicotine is addictive. Smokers need it to feel normal/calm.
- Nicotine alters the chemical balance in the brain and improves mood and concentration immediately.
- The body and mind get used to the effects and need more nicotine to get the same results, leading to addiction.

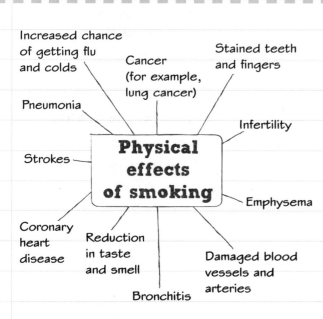

Physical effects of smoking:
- Increased chance of getting flu and colds
- Cancer (for example, lung cancer)
- Stained teeth and fingers
- Pneumonia
- Infertility
- Strokes
- Emphysema
- Coronary heart disease
- Reduction in taste and smell
- Damaged blood vessels and arteries
- Bronchitis

How patterns affect health

Children with three or more smokers in the household are two-and-a-half times more likely to smoke themselves, compared with children from non-smoking households (Source: Health and Social Care Information Centre, 2012).

Emotional and social effects

The emotional and social effects of smoking are:
- dependence
- worrying about money – cigarettes are expensive
- arguments with family and friends
- social isolation in public venues when needing to smoke
- feeling like an outcast.

Worked example

Which **two** of the following are health risks associated with smoking?   **(2 marks)**

A ☑ Lung cancer   B ☐ Liver disease
C ☐ Osteoporosis   D ☑ Emphysema
E ☐ Obesity

Look through all five answers and find the two that are to do with the **lungs**. Osteoporosis is to do with bones.

Now try this

Alena is 14 years old and has started smoking.

Give **two** reasons why Alena might have started smoking.   **(2 marks)**

To get full marks, you need to identify **two** reasons.

Recreational drug use

Recreational drugs may negatively affect your health and wellbeing. Drugs are chemicals that have an effect on the body. There are two types of drug.

 MEDICINAL DRUGS

- Drugs taken to control disease or pain
- Prescribed by a doctor or bought over the counter under controlled conditions
- Addictive if NOT taken under controlled conditions

 RECREATIONAL DRUGS

- Drugs that are taken for pleasure
- Can be legal or illegal:
  - Legal: tobacco, alcohol and caffeine
  - Illegal: for example cannabis, heroin, cocaine – taking, possessing or supplying these is against the law
- Can be addictive – as a person becomes more addicted, their consumption goes up, to try to get the same effect.

Different types of recreational drugs

Drug type	Examples	Possible effects	
		Short-term	Long-term
Stimulants – increase brain activity	Tobacco Caffeine Cocaine Amphetamines	More active Improved mood More energy Insomnia	Addiction Paranoia Aggressiveness Delusions
Depressants – decrease brain activity	Alcohol Solvents Barbiturates Heroin Cannabis	Drowsiness Calmness Reduced inhibition Reduced awareness Poor concentration	Addiction Breathing difficulties Sleep problems Sexual problems Mental health problems – anxiety Coma from overdose
Hallucinogens – cause hallucinations	LSD Ketamine MDMA	Changed impression of space and time Distorted senses Rapid mood swings	Addiction Lack of memory/ concentration Mental health problems – depression/panic Increased delusion

Possible effects of drugs

PHYSICAL

- ☒ Accidental death
- ☒ Illness and disease; for example, liver damage, HIV and hepatitis (from sharing needles/syringes)
- ☒ Impaired judgement leading to accident, injury or unsafe sexual practice

EMOTIONAL and SOCIAL

- ☒ Dependence
- ☒ Effects on mental health
- ☒ Loss of job
- ☒ Financial problems

Worked example

Damien has recently started taking drugs as a result of peer pressure.
State **two** possible long-term effects on his health and wellbeing.

(2 marks)

1 Impaired judgement causing him to do something dangerous.

2 Damien may develop mental health problems.

Now try this

Identify **one** way that experimenting with drugs can lead to mental health problems.

(1 mark)

Sexual practices

SAFE SEX can be emotionally rewarding. UNSAFE SEX can result in effects such as unwanted pregnancy and the spread of sexually transmitted infections.

Safe sexual practices

SAFE SEXUAL PRACTICES include:

- ✓ using contraception
- ✓ having sexual health check-ups
- ✓ only having sex with someone you trust
- ✓ limiting the number of sexual partners
- ✓ informing sexual partners of any sexually transmitted infections (STIs)
- ✓ not losing control of actions by taking drugs or drinking alcohol

Sexually transmitted infections

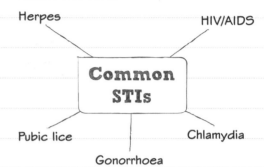

Herpes　　　　　　　　　　HIV/AIDS

Common
STIs

Pubic lice　　　　　　　　Chlamydia

Gonorrhoea

Symptoms of an STI

The most common symptoms of an STI are a discharge, pain or itching and a rash, blisters or sores.

Effects of unsafe sexual practice

PHYSICAL EFFECTS

- ✗ Getting and spreading STIs
- ✗ Related health risks – infertility, inflammatory pelvic disease
- ✗ Development of cervical cancer
- ✗ Unwanted pregnancy

EMOTIONAL AND SOCIAL EFFECTS

- ✗ Not developing close intimate and sexual relationships
- ✗ Break-up of relationships
- ✗ Loss of reputation and self-esteem

Number of sexual partners

If you have unsafe sex with someone who has had unsafe sex with lots of other partners, you have a higher risk of catching an STI.

Barrier contraception

BARRIER METHODS of contraception reduce the risk of STIs. They work by placing a barrier to prevent the sperm from reaching the egg.

Barrier methods include the following:

Condom – a rubber sheath that acts as a protective cover for the penis.

Female condom (femidom) – a rubber sheath that lines the vagina.

Diaphragm – a rubber cap that fits over the cervix.

Worked example

Explain **two** ways in which contraception can contribute to a healthy lifestyle.　**(2 marks)**

1　It can prevent unwanted pregnancies.

2　It can reduce the risk of getting STIs, which can lead to a range of other health problems.

Now try this

Name **two** possible effects of unprotected sex.　**(2 marks)**

Personal hygiene

Good personal hygiene is essential for good health. Poor personal hygiene can result in bad odours and infections.

Regular hand washing:
• after using the toilet
• before preparing food
• after sneezing

Bathing/showering

Using a tissue when coughing/sneezing

Throwing away food that falls on the floor

Examples of good personal hygiene

Brushing/combing your hair

Washing your hair regularly

Brushing your teeth regularly

Wearing clean clothes

Flushing the toilet

Possible effects of poor personal hygiene

PHYSICAL EFFECTS

(X) Catching disease/infections – for example, athlete's foot or diarrhoea

(X) Spread of disease and infections

(X) Body odour

(X) Bad breath

EMOTIONAL AND SOCIAL EFFECTS

(X) Loss of friends

(X) Social isolation

(X) Poor self-esteem, confidence and motivation

(X) Bullying

(X) Unemployment

Hand washing

Our hands are the most common way of transferring bacteria/viruses (for example, E. coli and streptococcus).

Regular HAND WASHING is essential to get rid of germs and prevent the spread of infections.

Good washing removes 99% of bacteria and viruses.

Alcohol-based hand sanitisers are often found in public places (such as hospitals) and should be used in addition to soap.

Preventing body odour

BATHING or SHOWERING and CHANGING YOUR CLOTHES will help prevent body odour.

You should do this at least once a day.

It is important to bath/shower after exercise, as sweat can cause you and your clothes to smell.

Worked example

Which **one** of the following is the main reason for washing your hands regularly? **(1 mark)**

A ☐ To prevent body odour

B ☐ To keep the nails clean

C ☑ To reduce germs

D ☐ To keep the hands clean

All these are good reasons for washing your hands, but you are being asked to pick the **most important** one.

Now try this

Give **two** ways in which poor personal hygiene may affect a person's health and wellbeing. **(2 marks)**

Sleep patterns

Getting enough sleep is a very important factor in a healthy lifestyle.

The sleep cycle

Sleep occurs in a recurring cycle of 90–110 minutes.

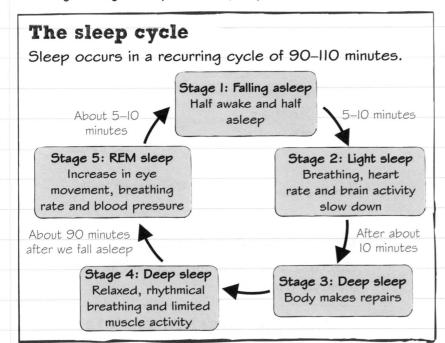

About 5–10 minutes

Stage 1: Falling asleep
Half awake and half asleep

5–10 minutes

Stage 5: REM sleep
Increase in eye movement, breathing rate and blood pressure

Stage 2: Light sleep
Breathing, heart rate and brain activity slow down

About 90 minutes after we fall asleep

After about 10 minutes

Stage 4: Deep sleep
Relaxed, rhythmical breathing and limited muscle activity

Stage 3: Deep sleep
Body makes repairs

The importance of regular sleep

✓ It allows the body to prepare itself for the next day by carrying out biological maintenance tasks.

✓ It keeps the brain healthy.

Most people need between 7.5 and 9 hours of sleep a day.

The quality of sleep affects all aspects of our daily life (for example, mental sharpness, productivity) as well as the age we might live to.

Effect of ageing on sleep

As we age, we:
- may find it harder to get to sleep
- may wake during sleep more often
- spend less time in deep, dreamless sleep, so may feel sleep-deprived
- are more likely to suffer from sleep disorders and insomnia.

Employment-related factors

✗ Jobs involving shift work make it difficult to sleep at regular times, so affect sleep patterns.

✗ People with stressful jobs may find it harder to get to sleep. Stress is a major cause of sleeping difficulties.

Physical and emotional effects of too little sleep

Poor attention span

May increase risk of obesity

Anxiety/ depression

Increased risk of accidents

Lack of sleep

Irritability

Lower energy levels

Stress and high blood pressure

Fatigue

Worked example

Sleep patterns change as we age.

Which **two** of the following are effects of ageing on sleep patterns? **(2 marks)**

A ☑ It may be harder to get to sleep

B ☑ Less time is spent in deep sleep

C ☐ More time is spent sleeping

D ☐ It is easier to get to sleep

E ☐ More time is spent in deep sleep

Now try this

Identify **two** ways in which having enough good-quality sleep can contribute to a healthy lifestyle. **(2 marks)**

Read the question carefully so you know whether you are being asked to give **positive** or **negative** points, or **both**. In this case, they will be positive.

Influences on lifestyles 1

The next four pages outline the factors that can affect your lifestyle choices. Some of the factors are out of your control.

Partners and family — Peer group pressure — Role models

Personal and family finances — **Influences on lifestyle choices** — Media influence

Culture and religion — Education and understanding

Genetic inheritance (including predisposition) — Mental health and illness — Self-esteem levels

Partners and family

PARTNERS/FAMILIES can influence choices about:

- what you eat
- what you wear
- how you speak
- healthcare (for example, whether you visit the dentist regularly)
- what you believe in/religion
- hobbies and interests
- attitudes towards others
- smoking and drinking.

Culture and religion

CULTURE and RELIGION may similarly affect lifestyle choices.

Example: Muslim beliefs

An observant Muslim may believe that:
- sex before marriage is wrong
- the family is the foundation of the community
- men should protect women
- women should dress modestly
- it is wrong to drink alcohol and use drugs
- it is unacceptable to eat pork.

Family: influence on drinking alcohol

If you see a family member getting drunk every week, you are more likely to think this is acceptable.

If your family allows you to drink alcohol at home under supervision, you are more likely to be aware of the effects of alcohol when drinking with your friends.

Your family's religious beliefs and ethnicity may influence whether you drink alcohol.

Worked example

Both of Ricky's parents have always smoked.

Explain **two** ways in which this might influence his decision on whether or not to smoke. **(4 marks)**

1 As Ricky's parents have smoked all his life, he may think it is an acceptable thing to do and copy them.

2 Ricky may have seen the negative effects of his parents' smoking, such as the cost, their smoker's cough and the fact that it makes their body, skin and hair smell. He may therefore decide not to smoke.

Now try this

State **two** ways in which a person's culture can influence their lifestyle choices. **(2 marks)**

It is often easier to state and then use an example of a culture when answering a question like this – for example, travellers.

Influences on lifestyles 2

It often feels important to fit in with a PEER GROUP, particularly during adolescence.

Friendships in adolescence

In adolescence, friendships become closer and even more influential than family relationships.

Adolescents also start forming intimate relationships.

Peer group pressure

PEER GROUP PRESSURE is the influence that people in a particular social group can have on other members of the group.

Positive peer group pressure

Positive peer group pressure gives positive encouragement and support. It will encourage you to think about the consequences of an action and make the right decisions.

- ✓ Not smoking, drinking alcohol or taking recreational drugs
- ✓ Encouraging others to stop smoking, drinking alcohol or taking recreational drugs
- ✓ Being polite and respectful of others and their property
- ✓ Working hard at school
- ✓ Treating others as you would like to be treated

Negative peer group pressure

Pressure from others in a group can sometimes result in negative outcomes – for example, doing things that are not safe or that others may disapprove of, even though it makes you feel uncomfortable.

- ✗ Pressure to try drugs, alcohol or cigarettes
- ✗ Pressure to have sex
- ✗ Stealing/ shoplifting
- ✗ Disrespect towards others and their property
- ✗ Pressure to dress in a certain way/ differently
- ✗ Playing truant from school
- ✗ Bullying others
- ✗ Staying up late

Pressure to smoke is an example of negative peer group pressure.

Worked example

Sameer has just moved to a new school and wants to fit in. Give **two** ways in which peer pressure could influence him to make a negative lifestyle choice. **(2 marks)**

1 His peers may smoke and he may feel that he needs to as well, in order to fit in.

2 His peers may cause trouble in class and expect him to join in, which will affect his chances of doing well at school.

Now try this

Which of the following is the correct definition of peer pressure?

A ☐ Pressure from your parents to act in a certain way

B ☐ Pressure that you put on yourself to behave in a certain way

C ☐ Pressure from other members of a social group to act in a certain way

D ☐ Pressure put on you by your teachers to behave in a certain way

Influences on lifestyles 3

Role models

ROLE MODELS are people who set an example and who influence our choices.

Attitudes, behaviours and skills can be learned from role models.

It is important to have good role models.

Good role models might be a family member, a teacher, a community leader/youth worker or someone in the public eye (for example, Jessica Ennis-Hill or Barack Obama).

What makes a good role model?

A good role model is usually:
- inspirational
- motivational
- trustworthy
- respectful of others
- true to their values/beliefs
- selfless and focuses on the good of others
- accepting of others
- able to overcome barriers.

Media influences

The MEDIA has a huge influence on lifestyle choices.

The media can influence:
- how we look
- how we behave
- what we eat
- the car we drive
- what we ASPIRE to
- how we feel about ourselves.

Key terms

ASPIRE: want to have or achieve something (such as a particular career or level of success)

THE MEDIA: different means of mass communication such as social network sites, magazines, the internet, TV, mobile phones and newspapers

Social media has a significant impact, both positive and negative, on our lifestyle.

Social media

Social media has many effects on us, including:

✓ keeping us in regular touch with one another

✓ allowing us to share images easily

✓ delivering messages on issues ranging from body image to whether to vaccinate babies.

✗ leading to a sedentary lifestyle

✗ leading to social isolation, as people communicate less face to face

✗ allowing cyber-bullying

✗ sometimes leading to contact with unsuitable people, causing danger.

Worked example

Give **two** ways in which a positive role model can influence lifestyle choices.   **(2 marks)**

1 A role model who is fit and active may inspire you to exercise more.

2 A role model who works hard will help you develop a good work ethic, so you are more likely to succeed at school and beyond.

Make sure you check if you are being asked about a **positive** or a **negative** role model.

Now try this

Identify **two** ways in which the media can influence a person to lead an unhealthy lifestyle.
(2 marks)

Influences on lifestyles 4

Self-esteem levels

Poor SELF-ESTEEM can have an effect on social and emotional wellbeing.

People with high self-esteem may be:

- ✓ more confident
- ✓ more successful
- ✓ more likely to seize opportunities.

Education and understanding

Better self-esteem

Better employment prospects

More opportunities to explore new ideas

More awareness of factors contributing to a healthy lifestyle

The effects of education on lifestyle

More likely to live longer

More opportunities to learn new skills

More career opportunities

Personal and family finances

Having enough money makes life less stressful, so it is easier to lead a happy, healthy lifestyle. Having enough income also makes it easier to:

- ✓ eat healthily
- ✓ go on holidays
- ✓ join a gym
- ✓ pay bills and mortgages
- ✓ enjoy social activities/hobbies
- ✓ buy nice clothes and go out
- ✓ relax with no money worries.

Genetic inheritance

Genes are inherited or passed down from our parents. Some genes that are inherited are faulty.

GENETIC INHERITANCE can therefore make us more likely to inherit certain diseases or conditions (this tendency is called predisposition).

Genetic inheritance, including predisposition, is out of our control, but influences our lifestyle choices.

Mental health and illness

MENTAL ILLNESS can be caused by:

- ✗ stress (for example, from money worries)
- ✗ relationship breakdowns
- ✗ substance abuse
- ✗ social isolation
- ✗ genetic inheritance.

Mental illness can be treated by prescription drugs or therapy, such as counselling.

Examples of mental health conditions

Depression, bipolar disorder, anxiety, obsessive compulsive disorder (OCD), phobias and a range of eating disorders, such as anorexia.

Worked example

Lina has just finished university and got a good job. She is fit and healthy and has high self-esteem.

Give **two** ways in which her high self-esteem level is likely to affect her lifestyle choices.   **(2 marks)**

1 She is likely to be more determined to be successful in her career.

2 She will have the confidence to seize new opportunities, such as joining a gym.

Make sure you read the question carefully. This is based on self-esteem rather than the other information given about Lina.

Now try this

State **two** reasons why a lack of education and understanding can sometimes lead to unhealthy lifestyle choices.   **(2 marks)**

Improving health and wellbeing 1

The first step in improving health and wellbeing is to identify areas for potential improvement. The second step is to draw up a healthy lifestyle plan to implement improvements.

Smoking

Work environment

Recreational drug use

 Alcohol consumption

 Exercise

Possible areas for improvement

 Home environment

 Personal hygiene

 Diet

 Sexual practices

Implementation

To improve an area of your health and wellbeing, you need to start by drawing up a plan. A good health plan should include:
- the problem(s) to be tackled
- goals (long-term aims) and targets (short-term challenges) – including benefits and methods of meeting each target
- alternative strategies, to overcome any difficulties that may arise
- dates for regular monitoring and reviewing of targets
- longer-term strategies for maintaining improvements.

What is the target?

The target needs to be stated clearly and concisely, and in a way that allows you to measure progress. For example:
- ✗ 'I want to change the way I eat' is too vague.
- ✓ 'I intend to lose 1 stone in weight by my birthday on 10 December' is specific and leaves no room for misunderstanding or excuses.

Targets should be SMART. More information on SMART targets is on page 65.

The statement needs to be **specific**. It should include a goal and details of how and when he will achieve the goal.

Worked example

Identify **two** features of a successful health improvement plan. **(2 marks)**

1 Targets
2 Strategies to meet the targets

Now try this

Yohan has decided to improve his fitness. His goal is to do a 10k fun run next year. He has drawn up a health improvement plan.

Which **one** of the following statements is the most clear and specific, and should be included in his plan? **(1 mark)**

A ☐ I want to get fit by running regularly
B ☐ I want to get fit and do a 10k fun run in the summer
C ☐ I want to improve my fitness
D ☐ I want to get fit so that I can do a 10k fun run on 21 May next year

62

Improving health and wellbeing 2

A health plan should also include identifying any difficulties so you can overcome these.

Getting started

It is very easy to put off starting the change to a healthier lifestyle. Excuses for not starting a weight loss diet today might include:

- ✗ I haven't got the right food in my home.
- ✗ The battery in my scales is flat.
- ✗ It's too cold to diet.
- ✗ I'm too stressed.
- ✗ I'm too busy to think about it.
- ✗ Another day won't hurt – I'll start tomorrow.
- ✗ I'll probably give up, so I may as well not try.

Benefits

Instead of thinking of excuses, it is better to think about the BENEFITS of a healthier lifestyle. For example:

- ✓ weight loss
- ✓ reduced risk of diseases such as heart disease and cancer
- ✓ reduced risk of conditions such as high blood pressure
- ✓ improved fitness, confidence and self-esteem
- ✓ feeling happier
- ✓ access to more life opportunities.

Example: weight loss

Someone who is 50 kg (nearly 8 stone) overweight is realistically going to take over a year to lose the extra weight. This may seem impossible. It is better to set an initial mini goal of losing 10 kg (about 1.5 stone) in four months. This goal is also SMART.

Setting realistic goals and targets

TARGETS and GOALS must be realistic so that you can achieve them without giving up.

Appropriate weight loss on a diet is 0.5 to 1 kg a week (1 to 2 lbs a week), this may be after the initial larger loss due to losing lots of water.

Seeking support

Support to help live a healthier lifestyle may come from:

- family
- friends
- work colleagues
- healthcare professionals
- voluntary services
- health promotion materials.

Accessing professional help

PROFESSIONAL HELP can be free or paid for (private). Professional weight loss help might come from a:

- doctor
- slimming club
- counsellor
- dietician
- hypnotherapist.

Worked example

Identify **two** things you need to do when drawing up a health plan. **(2 marks)**

1 Set realistic goals

2 Seek support

Now try this

Franco smokes 40 cigarettes a day and wants to stop smoking.

1 Explain how **one** source of support he could seek could help him. **(2 marks)**

2 Give **one** example of a realistic goal Franco could set for stopping smoking. **(1 mark)**

Improving health and wellbeing 3

Other potential difficulties that need to be considered before starting a health plan are TIME COMMITMENT and MOTIVATION.

Time commitment

If you are trying to exercise more, you need to:

- set aside regular time to exercise
- balance exercise and home life commitments
- balance exercise and work commitments
- identify and manage times when you are likely to find it difficult to stick to the plan, such as:
  - when it's dark, cold and wet outside
  - when you're ill
  - times of the year when your social life is more hectic – for example, Christmas.

Not enough time? Make some!

- Get up 30 minutes earlier to exercise.
- Arrange to meet a friend to exercise so you don't find an excuse not to do it.
- Build exercise into your daily routine – walk or cycle short distances, such as going to school or college, or get off the bus earlier.
- Walk upstairs instead of taking lifts or escalators.
- Exercise while watching TV – for example, do some yoga poses, squats, lunges or planks during the adverts.
- Exercise at home using a DVD – for example, yoga, home workouts, martial arts.
- Join a team so that you are committed to going and not letting other team members down.

Motivation

MOTIVATION is needed not only to start a health plan but also to stick to it. To remain motivated, it is important to think about the following.

- BENEFITS – Keep thinking about the benefits (for example, being able to fit into smaller clothes, losing weight).
- VARIETY – Vary exercise routines and diet to prevent boredom and for enjoyment (for example, do a Zumba class as well as running).
- REWARDS – Include rewards – for example, 'If I can run a mile without stopping I can download a new album from iTunes.' Try to make sure that the rewards don't undo the good work already done – for example, cakes and biscuits may not be good rewards for someone wanting to lose weight.
- GOALS – Set yourself a realistic goal, such as running a 10k race, and ask friends to sponsor you so you can't back out.

Worked example

Explain why it is important to balance exercise and other commitments.   **(2 marks)**

1 If you spend all your time at the gym, you may fall behind with your studies.

2 You may also not see your family and friends as much, and this may cause strain on relationships.

You can easily build exercise into your daily routine but this question asks you to think about how to **balance** your other commitments.

Now try this

Gillie wants to give up drinking.

Explain **two** ways in which she could motivate herself to carry on even when she is craving alcohol.   **(4 marks)**

Improving health and wellbeing 4

For a health plan to succeed, it is crucial to set SMART TARGETS.

SMART targets

Targets must be:

- **S**PECIFIC – the target must state an exact goal, so it is clear and can't be misunderstood
- **M**EASURABLE – the target can be measured to show you have met it
- **A**CHIEVABLE – it must be possible to achieve the target so you don't give up
- **R**EALISTIC – the target must be sensible so you can achieve it
- **T**IME-RELATED – the target must have a deadline date for achievement.

Setting SMART targets will help you achieve your goals.

This table shows some of the differences between SMART and vague targets.

Vague targets	SMART targets
Eat more healthily	Eat five portions of fruit and vegetables a day
Exercise more	Exercise for 30 minutes five days a week
Lose one stone in weight	Lose at least 1 lb a week for 14 weeks
Drink less alcohol	Cut down the amount of alcohol I drink by five units a week
Smoke fewer cigarettes	Smoke ten fewer cigarettes each day
Give up taking drugs	Seek professional advice and put together a health plan for managing my withdrawal in the next week
Have safe sex	Use a barrier method of contraception every time I have sex
Be cleaner	Wash and clean my teeth twice a day and change my underwear every day

Short-, medium- and long-term targets

A health plan should have SHORT-TERM, MEDIUM-TERM and LONG-TERM targets.

- Short-term targets may be achieved in a week or two.
- Medium-term targets may be achieved in a month or two.
- Long-term targets may be achieved in six months to a year (or longer).

Worked example

Which **two** of the following are examples of SMART targets? **(2 marks)**

A ☐ I will have skimmed milk in my tea rather than semi-skimmed

B ☑ I will take a packed lunch to college three days this week rather than buying lunch

C ☐ I will go for a walk with a friend for 15 minutes

D ☑ I will walk for half an hour every day this week after college

E ☐ I will lose weight

Now try this

Elesha wants to cut down on the amount of drugs she takes.
Write **one** SMART target for Elesha and explain why it is SMART. **(2 marks)**

Try to think of a different target from the one in the table above.

Improving health and wellbeing 5

INTERVENTION STRATEGIES are ways that you can improve health and wellbeing. They are an important part of a healthy lifestyle plan. Below are some examples of different types of intervention strategies that you can use to stop smoking.

Healthy lifestyle plan and intervention strategies

You have already looked at healthy lifestyle plans over the last four pages. The first line of a typical healthy lifestyle plan is given below:

BENEFITS of meeting the targets provide motivation (for example, financial benefits from reduced expenditure as well as health benefits)

TARGETS need to be SMART (see page 65)

The COST of strategies needs to be considered to make sure they are affordable:
• paid-for aids – patches, gum and e-cigarettes
• free sources – support groups, willpower, online support

Problem to be tackled: To stop smoking. Currently smokes 20 cigarettes a day.

Date	Target	Benefits	Support strategies	Alternative strategies	Costs	Notes
Week 1	Cut down from 20 cigarettes a day to 15	Blood pressure will go down. Save money	Nicotine patches. Leaflets on giving up smoking	E-cigarettes	Patches E-cigarettes	

SUPPORT STRATEGIES for meeting the targets such as:
• NRT (nicotine replacement therapy) including nicotine patches, gum, lozenges, and nasal sprays
• SUPPORT SERVICES such as:
  ○ NHS Stop Smoking Service – NHS helpline
  ○ Smokefree Together Programme – provides advice and 'quit kits'
  ○ e-cigarettes
  ○ text support services
  ○ online support – Change4Life
  ○ local face-to-face support groups
  ○ hypnotherapy

ALTERNATIVE STRATEGIES in case the original strategy isn't working, for example:
• the adhesive on nicotine patches may irritate your skin and you may prefer to use gum
• it may be more motivating to attend a support group rather than get online support
• it may be more convenient to speak to someone on the phone rather than face to face

Tip
The plan could be presented in a way that means it can be put on the wall as a constant reminder.

Worked example

Jaydon is trying to cut down his excessive alcohol consumption. He has done well for the first two weeks by having a soft drink every other drink and by reminding himself of the health benefits. However, he is now struggling to cut down further.

Suggest **one** alternative strategy he could use and explain how he would use it. **(3 marks)**

Jaydon could avoid triggers, so instead of meeting his friends in a bar, he could suggest they try something else instead, such as paintballing or jogging. He would then be in an environment that is not associated with alcohol, and this would help take his mind off alcohol.

There are many strategies for cutting down on alcohol, but as the question only asks for **one**, pick one that you can **explain**.

Now try this

Give **two** reasons why it is important to include the benefits of meeting each target on a health plan. **(2 marks)**

Improving health and wellbeing 6

Other intervention strategies include HYPNOTHERAPY and ACUPUNCTURE, as well as specific techniques to reduce alcohol consumption or drug use.

Hypnotherapy

Hypnotherapy uses hypnosis to alter a person's state of consciousness and relax them. Once relaxed, the hypnotist uses the power of suggestion to help overcome the problem.

It doesn't work for everyone, but it does seem to have a positive effect on some people.

Hypnotherapy can be used to help overcome phobias and to help meet targets, such as weight loss and stopping smoking.

Acupuncture

Acupuncture is a form of ancient Chinese medicine. Some people believe that illness results from imbalances in energy flows.

Fine needles are inserted into the skin at certain points on the body. The needles stimulate points in the body to correct the energy imbalances and help illness.

Techniques for reducing alcohol consumption

- ✓ Keep track of alcohol consumption by writing it down.
- ✓ Have:
  - ◦ drink-free days
  - ◦ smaller drinks
  - ◦ lower-strength drinks
  - ◦ soft drinks
  - ◦ tea or coffee instead.
- ✓ Offer to be the driver.
- ✓ Use online/face-to-face support groups.
- ✓ Work out how much it is costing you to drink.

Acupuncture can help rebalance the energy flows in the body, which some believe is essential for good health.

Techniques for reducing recreational drug use

- ✓ Keep track of drug use by writing it down.
- ✓ List the pros and cons of quitting.
- ✓ Consider the effects on family and friends.
- ✓ Attend a support group.
- ✓ Find friends who don't use drugs.
- ✓ Exercise more.

Worked example

Tomas wants to reduce his recreational drug use. Explain how a face-to-face support group could help him. **(2 marks)**

Talking to others who may have already reduced their own use means that:
- Tomas can learn about the strategies they used
- he may feel he is with people who understand and can support him better.

Now try this

Explain how **one** example of an intervention strategy for reducing alcohol consumption can help. **(2 marks)**

67

Formal support

The support available to help promote healthy lifestyles can be divided into FORMAL SUPPORT and INFORMAL SUPPORT. Informal support is covered on the following page.

Sources of formal support

Formal support is given by someone who has been trained and is usually paid to give that support. Examples include doctors, health specialists, counsellors and personal trainers.

For young people

Youth workers, teachers and career advisers offer formal advice and guidance to young people.

They can offer advice on areas of personal development, such as fitness, personal hygiene, safe sex, smoking, drugs and alcohol. They can also advise about career options, either within lessons or through programmes or small group sessions.

For working adults

Human resources departments offer adults in their workplace support on:
- occupational health, if ill health is affecting work
- personal and career development
- equality, diversity and rights
- work-related issues, such as stress
- health and safety.

Employee assistance programmes (EAPs)

Some employers offer EAPs to help employees deal with issues that may affect their work performance, health and wellbeing. For example, they may provide counselling about recreational drug use, finances or health.

Alcohol (for example, Alcoholics Anonymous)
HIV/AIDS (for example, Terrence Higgins Trust)
STIs (for example, Society of Sexual Health Advisers)
Cigarettes (for example, QUIT)
Skin and hair (for example, National Eczema Society and Alopecia UK)
Fitness (for example, Change4Life)

Types of formal support groups

Eating disorders (for example, B-eat)
Lifestyle (for example, Teenage Health Freak)
Slimming groups (for example, Weight Watchers)
Drugs (for example, Action on Addiction)
Health promotion (for example, Action on Smoking and Health)

Worked example

Arthur is obese.

Identify **one** source of formal support Arthur could access, and explain how it could help him achieve a healthier lifestyle. **(3 marks)**

Arthur could see a dietician, who could give him advice on a weight loss diet, suggest strategies to help him stick to the diet and monitor his progress.

Make sure you identify the **source** of formal support and then **explain** how the source will help Arthur.

Now try this

Using an example of a particular lifestyle issue, explain **two** ways in which a teacher can provide formal support about a healthier lifestyle for young people. **(4 marks)**

Informal support

Informal support is usually not provided by an organised group, or by a trained, paid professional.

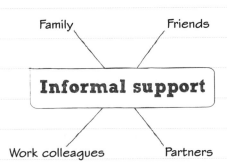

These people aren't paid to offer informal support. They do it because they care and feel they have a duty to help.

Family

For many people, family is the largest form of informal support.

Lifestyle change	Family support
Eat more healthily	All members of the family have a similar healthy eating plan.
Lose weight	The rest of the family eats low-fat meals.
Do more exercise	A family member no longer gives you a lift to school, or they drop you off further away so you can walk.
Improve emotional wellbeing	Other family members offer to listen to your worries and concerns.

Friends

FRIENDS are an extremely important source of informal support.

Lifestyle change	You could ask friends to...
Drink less alcohol	offer to buy you soft drinks instead.
Stop taking drugs	help you find support groups and be there to talk to when you need a distraction.
Smoke less	refuse to give you a cigarette or lend you money.
Improve emotional wellbeing	be there for you to talk to.

Partners

PARTNERS can give support by:
- following a health plan for eating healthily, exercising or stopping smoking
- praising you and encouraging you not to give up
- complimenting you about any improvement
- reassuring you if you have a bad day.

Partners can give encouragement by joining in.

Which **two** of the following are sources of informal support?   **(2 marks)**

A ☑ Family

B ☐ Counselling services

C ☐ Healthcare professionals

D ☑ Friends

E ☐ Social workers

Read the question carefully to see which type of support it is asking about. In this case, it is **informal** support.

Now try this

Using an example of a particular lifestyle change, outline the difference between formal and informal support.   **(4 marks)**

69

Support in maintaining positive change

Both formal and informal support in maintaining a positive lifestyle change can come in the form of LISTENING, EMPATHY, ENCOURAGEMENT or ADVICE and GUIDANCE.

Keeping to the plan

To stick to the plan, use the following.

INFORMAL SUPPORT

- Keep family and friends informed about targets, and ask for their continued support.
- Keep family and friends informed of progress, so they can give praise and encouragement to continue with the good work.
- Put the plan somewhere visible, so that everyone can look at it daily to track progress.
- Keep family and friends informed of needs, such as needs for particular foods.

FORMAL SUPPORT

- Get details of support services, such as telephone helplines or support groups.

Maintaining positive change

Ongoing support is needed to maintain a positive lifestyle change once the goal has been achieved. For example, the following support would be needed to maintain weight loss:

- formal support – advice and guidance on how to keep the weight off from a dietician
- informal support – continued support and encouragement from family by:
  - sticking to a healthier way of eating
  - continuing to buy healthy food
- support and understanding from friends so they don't tempt you to eat and drink the wrong things.

Maintaining a positive outlook

It is easy to get disheartened and bored once the initial feelings of determination and pleasure at making progress start to wear off.

For example, losing weight can happen quickly at the start of a diet, but then might slow down after a few weeks.

Encouragement from others is essential to maintain a positive outlook.

Key term

EMPATHY: being able to understand and share the feelings of the person you are listening to

Exercising with a friend can help to encourage each other.

Worked example

This question asks you to 'explain'. This tells you that you need to state **two** ways Jenny can use family support and then explain **both** to get full marks.

Jenny has decided to lose weight.

Explain **two** ways in which support from her family could help her to lose weight.   **(4 marks)**

1 If all the members of Jenny's family agree to eat more healthily, she won't feel as though she is missing out as much.

2 If her family praises her achievements, it will encourage her to stick to her eating plan.

Now try this

Explain **two** ways in which family and friends can support maintenance of a healthier lifestyle.

(4 marks)

Pick an aspect of a healthier lifestyle, such as more exercise, to help you answer this question.

Barriers to health 1

There are a number of factors that may restrict you from leading a healthy lifestyle.

Financial limitations

A lack of money will influence the choices you can make. For example, it may influence food choices. But even with a limited budget you can still make healthy food choices.

Frozen/tinned fruit and vegetables
• Cheaper than fresh produce
• Less waste

Tinned oily fish
• Cheaper than fresh fish
• Still contains omega-3 fats
• Long shelf life

Measure your portion sizes – saves money

Freeze leftovers from other meals

Limited budget

Shop in the market, not supermarket - cheaper and often fresher

Eat seasonal fruit and vegetables – produce is cheaper in season

Make your own lunches
• Cheaper than buying it
• Can control calories

Use less meat and more vegetables in dishes

Genetic factors and current physical condition

These can restrict lifestyle choices, such as the exercise someone can do or the diet they can follow. The person might:
• find it hard to access services, due to a physical disability
• not be able to access information, due to a sight or hearing impairment
• feel they can't change because they are too embarrassed to try.

To overcome these barriers:
• health professionals can give advice, guidance and support
• the person can join a support group
• someone who is exercising for weight loss can start by exercising sitting down.

Finding resources and support

In an isolated rural area, it may be more difficult to access resources and support. For example, a regular shopping trip may not be possible so planning a weekly shop for the correct foods will be crucial.

Time limitations

Life can be very busy and it may be hard to find time to make changes – see page 65.

Unrealistic goals

Targets and goals must be realistic so that a person sees that they can be achieved and isn't tempted to give up – see page 65.

Worked example

Shamma is 23 years old and has had mobility problems since she was in a car accident when she was 14. She wants to lose weight, but finds it very hard to exercise. She enjoys a drink or meal with friends at the weekend, and watches television for relaxation. She works in an office all day, using a computer and phone.

Identify **two** factors that are limiting Shamma's chances of losing weight.   **(2 marks)**

1 Her social life mainly involves eating and drinking with friends

2 Her sedentary work

Remember to **identify**, and then **explain**, two barriers.

Now try this

Explain how Shamma could overcome **two** barriers that are stopping her achieving a healthy lifestyle.   **(4 marks)**

Barriers to health 2

Other BARRIERS to achieving a healthy lifestyle include the influence of others, such as partners, family, peer group and the media.

Influence of partners and family

A person's partner and family might be unsupportive by:

- ☒ not also agreeing to adopt a healthy lifestyle (for example, not doing exercise)
- ☒ making unhealthy choices (for example, cooking unhealthy meals or ordering a takeaway)
- ☒ putting temptations in the way, such as bringing home a bottle of wine when someone is trying to cut down on alcohol
- ☒ encouraging unsafe sex
- ☒ smoking or drinking alcohol.

This makes it much harder to maintain motivation.

Peer group pressure

Negative **peer group pressure** can put temptation in the way of achieving a healthy lifestyle.

Media influence

The MEDIA can show unhealthy lifestyle choices and make people aim for unrealistic goals.

Images of the body: for example, thin models/celebrities

Adverts: for example, TV adverts for unhealthy food

TV: drinking and smoking on soaps/reality shows

Inactivity: spending more time watching TV/on games/social media and less time being active

Magazine articles: for example, on celebrity diet crazes with unrealistic goals or how to achieve an unhealthy weight

Worked example

Joey has recently stopped drinking alcohol. All his friends still drink on a regular basis.

Identify **two** ways in which peer pressure and other influences may be barriers to a healthy lifestyle for Joey.

(2 marks)

1 He may feel pressure to start drinking again to fit into his friendship group.
2 Friends and family may put temptations in his way by offering or buying him alcoholic drinks.

Now try this

Identify **two** barriers related to giving up recreational drugs.

(2 marks)

Barriers to health 3

Further barriers to achieving a healthy lifestyle include a lack of MOTIVATION to change and low SELF-ESTEEM.

Motivation to change

It is easy to find motivation at the start of a new lifestyle change, but over time it gets harder to maintain that motivation.

Lack of confidence/self-esteem: it is easier to stay the same rather than change

Lack of incentives to make changes

Lack of desire to change: for example, the person may not want to lose weight/give up smoking

Lack of progress: for example, weight loss may slow down after initial progress

Reasons motivation may be hard

Conflict between two choices: for example, giving up smoking might result in weight gain

Negative attitude: for example, focusing on the negative (what they haven't achieved) rather than the positive (what they have achieved)

Lack of priority: there may be other things that interfere or that they want to do instead

Case study

Kate is a professional dancer, but six months ago she suffered a serious knee injury. She has already put on weight as she is no longer dancing every day. She is very disheartened, as she fears this is the end of her dancing career and she has no idea what she will do for work if so.

Kate now has low self-esteem and no motivation to lose weight.

Motivation is within our control. It doesn't take much to make a change. Without motivation, it is hard to change.

Self-esteem

People with low self-esteem don't think much of themselves. They may feel that:

- ⊗ they can't change
- ⊗ there is no point, because others won't notice
- ⊗ they are no good at anything and so can't change
- ⊗ no one will want to support them or help them.

Worked example

Misha is 25 years old and has low self-esteem due to a skin complaint that regularly flares up, leaving red blotches on his face. He drinks heavily at the weekend with his friends. He knows he needs to cut down on his drinking for the sake of his health, but he drinks because the alcohol makes him more relaxed and confident, so he has no motivation to change.

Identify **two** barriers to Misha achieving a healthy lifestyle.

(2 marks)

1 His social life

2 His low self-esteem

Now try this

Explain **two** reasons why Misha finds it hard to find motivation to make the changes needed to achieve a healthy lifestyle.   **(4 marks)**

To answer this question, refer back to the case study in the worked example.

Barriers to health 4

The final barriers to achieving a healthy lifestyle are LACK OF EDUCATION, ADDICTION and AVAILABILITY of negative lifestyle choices.

Lack of education and understanding

A lack of education can result in a lack of knowledge and understanding about lifestyle choices and how to make changes.

Addiction

Addiction is very hard to break.

Addiction to drugs, for example, causes changes to the brain, which make it harder to think clearly and create cravings.

Support and willpower are essential in overcoming addiction.

Availability of negative lifestyle choices

Fast food and cheap alcohol seem to be available everywhere, so temptation is always in the way. This makes it harder to find the motivation to make lifestyle changes.

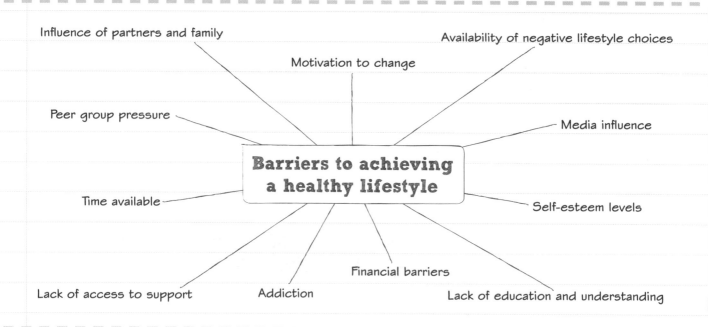

Influence of partners and family

Motivation to change

Availability of negative lifestyle choices

Peer group pressure

Media influence

Barriers to achieving a healthy lifestyle

Time available

Self-esteem levels

Lack of access to support

Addiction

Financial barriers

Lack of education and understanding

Worked example

Which **two** of the following barriers to health are within a person's control?   **(2 marks)**

A ☑ Addiction

B ☐ Genetic inheritance

C ☑ Lack of education

D ☐ Availability of negative lifestyle choices

E ☐ Peer group pressure

Now try this

Kristina is addicted to recreational drugs.

Explain **two** reasons why Kristina's addiction is a barrier to achieving a healthy lifestyle.

(4 marks)

Remember that you get 2 marks for **identifying** the reasons and 2 marks for **explaining** them.

Exam skills 1

Your exam will last 1 hour and the total number of marks available to you is 50. The total number of marks for each question is shown in brackets, so make sure you have made enough different points to earn them.

Use of numbers

In this exam you will be expected to be able to use numbers correctly when asked to calculate and analyse a person's BMI. Make sure that you show all your working out.

Hint

You will be given a person's height in metres and weight in kg and the formula for BMI. However, it is important that you learn the formula and practise working it out, so you are totally comfortable using it.

If your answer is somewhere between about 15 and 45, your maths is correct. If your answer is much smaller or bigger, then you need to check your working out, as you will have made a mistake.

Steps to calculate BMI

Health professionals sometimes use a chart like this to work out BMI. You will need to use a calculator.

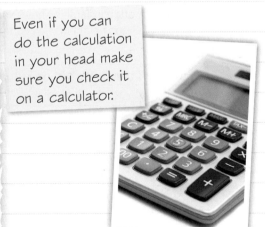

Remember that the formula is:

$$BMI = \frac{(\text{Weight in kg})}{(\text{Height in metres})^2}$$

It is important that you follow these steps in the correct order.

1 Square the height in metres (multiply the height by itself).

2 Divide the weight in kg by the number you got when you squared the height. If in doubt, remember that you will be dividing a bigger number by a smaller number.

Write the answer on the line provided. The unit is usually given, but if it isn't, remember to add it. It is kg/m^2.

Worked example

A typical question will have two parts. We will look at part (a) first.

(a) The information in Table A shows some details of Suzanne's height and weight.

Table A

Height (in m)	Weight (in kg)
1.6	55

Calculate Suzanne's Body Mass Index (BMI). Show your working out. **(2 marks)**

BMI = <u> 21.5 kg/m² </u> kg/m²

$$BMI = \frac{\text{Weight in kg}}{(\text{Height in m})^2}$$

$$BMI = \frac{55}{1.6^2}$$

$$BMI = \frac{55}{2.56}$$

Even if you can do the calculation in your head make sure you check it on a calculator.

You must show your working out in the space provided. If you work out the answer on your calculator and write only the answer on the exam paper, you will lose the mark allocated for the working out, even if you get the answer right. The first mark is for your working out, and the other mark is for the correct answer.

Exam skills 2

The second part of a typical question on BMI will ask you to explain what the BMI you have just worked out tells you about the person's weight.

Worked example

(b) Using Suzanne's BMI result, select her BMI rating using Table B.   **(1 mark)**

Table B

BMI	Rating
<19	Underweight
20–25	Desirable
25–30	Overweight
31+	Obese

Put a cross in **one** box ☒ to indicate your answer. If you change your mind, put a line through the box ☒ and then put a cross in another box ☒.

A ☐ Underweight

B ☒ Desirable

C ☐ Overweight

D ☐ Obese

On the previous page, we worked out that Suzanne's BMI is 21.5 kg/m². Comparing this figure with the table, this shows that her BMI falls within the 'Desirable' rating, so you would put your X in the box next to 'B Desirable'.

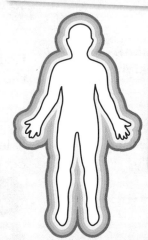

Colour	Rating
Yellow	Underweight
Green	Desirable
Blue	Overweight
Red	Obese

It is important that you **don't** learn any BMI table off by heart. These vary slightly, so it is important to use the one given on the exam paper, in this case Table B.

Now try this

(a) The information in Table A shows some details of Gino's height and weight.

Table A

Height (in m)	Weight (in kg)
1.7	80

Calculate Gino's Body Mass Index (BMI).

Show your working out in the space below.   **(2 marks)**

BMI = _____ kg/m²

(b) Using Gino's BMI result, select his BMI rating using Table B.

Table B

BMI	Rating
<19	Underweight
20–25	Desirable
25–30	Overweight
31+	Obese

Put a cross in **one** box ☒ to indicate your answer. If you change your mind, put a line through the box ☒ and then put a cross in another box ☒.   **(1 mark)**

A ☐ Underweight

B ☐ Desirable

C ☐ Overweight

D ☐ Obese

Exam skills 3

Objective questions

The Unit 9 exam will contain brief objective questions. These will test your knowledge of a part of the unit and use command words such as 'give', 'state' or 'identify'.

Make sure you give the number of effects asked for, in this case **two**.

Read the question carefully. This one asks for a **negative** effect, so make sure that is what you give.

Worked example

Regular exercise is an important part of a healthy lifestyle.

(a) Give **two** effects of regular exercise. **(2 marks)**

1 Maintain healthy weight
2 Improve suppleness

(b) Identify **one** way in which a person's job can have a negative effect on how often they exercise. **(1 mark)**

Working long hours may make the person too tired to exercise.

Short answer questions

These need more explanation to show your understanding of part of a topic, rather than just knowing it.

Worked example

Shaun is 18 years old and enjoys socialising with his friends at weekends. He binge drinks on a regular basis each weekend.

(a) Describe **one** way in which binge drinking can lead to an increased risk of an accident.
  (2 marks)

As Shaun drinks, he will lose track of what he is consuming and may drink more or stronger alcohol than he intended, leading to him being unsteady on his feet and losing inhibition or judgement.

This may result in Shaun becoming reckless or careless, and he will therefore be more likely to have an accident, such as falling off a balcony or walking into the road in front of a car.

The word 'describe' means that you have to give reasons **why** he gives in to peer pressure, rather than just saying his peers will encourage him.

Worked example

(b) Describe how peer influence may have led to Shaun drinking alcohol. **(2 marks)**

It is important to Shaun to be accepted by his peers. If they drink and encourage him to join in, he may do so in order to be part of the group.

He may also want to be seen as someone who defies authority and is a bit of a rebel, in order to impress others in his peer group.

There are two marks for part (a), so you need to write two sentences making two different points to explain (i) drinking too much and (ii) how an accident might happen.

Now try this

Kylie is 14 years old and smokes 20 cigarettes a day. Explain how her peers could help her to give up smoking.
  (2 marks)

Had a look ☐   Nearly there ☐   Nailed it! ☐

Exam skills 4

In an extended writing question, you will need to provide detailed information, usually based on information given in a case study.

Extended writing questions tips

✓ Read the case study very carefully.

✓ Read the question asked very carefully.

✓ Identify the command words – for example, 'evaluate' or 'assess', which would mean that you are being asked to give your opinion based on the positive and negative points being made.

✓ Read the case study again, bearing in mind the command words you have just identified and what the question is asking.

✓ Underline or highlight any key, relevant points.

✓ Think about – or better still, sketch out – some ideas for a plan before you start writing your answer.

✓ Use all the space given for the answer.

✓ Write in complete sentences.

✓ Answer the question based on the information given in the case study.

✗ Do not write about a different situation.

Worked example

Read the information about Sheona below. Sheona is 34 years old and is married with three children. She works part time as a hotel receptionist. At work, Sheona is seated for most of the day. When she leaves work, she collects her children from school by car. In the evening she likes to relax in front of the television, with a glass of wine. At the weekend, Sheona enjoys meals out with friends and family.

Sheona is unhappy with her weight. She has gained over 5 kg in the last year and now weighs 85 kg. Although she has lost weight before, she has always put it back on and so struggles with motivation. Sheona has set herself a target of losing 20 kg in the next six months.

Evaluate how likely it is that Sheona will meet her target. **(8 marks)**

> What could she **do** to lose weight?

Sheona could devise or download a weight loss diet, with SMART targets, and could join a slimming club or seek support from her doctor in order to lose weight. This support will help her to avoid putting the weight back on. She may find it hard to motivate herself to change her social life, which revolves around food and drink. She could walk to collect the children from school if time allows, or change her social life so that it includes either exercise or some other activity that does not involve eating. To help with this, she could ask her friends to help her by also going on a diet or cooking low-fat meals, so that they can encourage each other. By doing this, Sheona is incorporating exercise and a healthy diet into her current lifestyle. Because these changes will be part of her everyday routine she is more likely to not lose motivation and so lose weight.

> What are the potential **barriers** to her losing weight?

Sheona's children keep her occupied and this may interfere with her plans by stopping her going shopping for the healthy food items she needs. However, if Sheona has the support of her husband then he can help with childcare, giving her time to shop. She may have low self-esteem because of her weight and so may not want to walk or exercise in front of other people. Also, her friends and husband may not want to make these changes so she may find it hard without their support. However, if Sheona uses some, or all, of these strategies then she could be successful in losing the weight.

Answers

The following pages contain answers to the 'Now try this' questions in Unit 1 of the Revision Guide.

Learning aim A

1. The six life stages

Angie is in the **middle adulthood** life stage.
Jake is in the **early childhood** life stage.
Geoff is in the **later adulthood** life stage.

2. Aspects of development

Physical growth

3. Growth and physiological change

Physical growth – suggested answers could include:
- growing taller
- growing heavier
- increase in head circumference.

Physiological change – suggested answers could include:
- developing physical skills, gaining strength and muscle tone
- sexual maturity/puberty
- ageing process (for example, menopause/hair loss)
- loss of skills, sensory loss, loss of muscle tone.

4. Gross motor skills

1 and 2 Suggested answers could include:

Gross motor skill	Activity
Stand for a few moments	Push-and-pull toys
Crawl	Balls to push/crawl after
Use muscles in legs to pull themselves up	Ride-on toys

5. Fine motor skills

C The development of movement of the small muscles of the fingers and hands

6. Physical development in adolescence

Primary sexual characteristics refer to the reproductive organs, which are present from birth and develop during puberty. Secondary sexual characteristics are the other changes that happen to adolescents' bodies during puberty as a result of hormones being released.

7. Physical development in adulthood

Any two from the following: reach full height and strength; development of sexual characteristics; are able to reproduce; women are at their most fertile.

8. Intellectual development

A Joining a reading group
C Learning a foreign language

9. Language development

Suggested answers could include: sharing a story book and playing with puppets.

10. Moral development

Suggested answers could include:
- When Ajay and his friends have agreed rules, they are more likely to remember and follow them.
- Ajay and his friends will remind one another of the rules that they understand.

11. Emotional development

Suggested answers could include:
- Ashton may develop strong bonds and attachments with his parents or carer.
- Ashton will feel contented when his needs, such as love, food and warmth, are met.
- Ashton will feel happy and will not get distressed.

12. Social development

- When children are less dependent on their parents, they are more likely to socialise with others.
- If children are independent and confident, they are more likely to take part in activities and meet people.

13. Emotional and social development in infancy

- Infants have strong bonds with their parents and are reluctant to be looked after by other people.
- They rely on parents for all their needs, such as love, food and warmth.

14. Emotional and social development in early childhood

Suggested answers could include:
- Because Jodie lacks independence, she may have difficulty in taking part in social play or interacting with other children.
- Because Jodie finds it difficult to control her emotions, she may have difficulty in sharing and taking turns with other children.
- Jodie's ability to make friends may be affected because her lack of independence has given her a negative self-image, which will affect her confidence.
- Because Jodie becomes easily frustrated, the other children may isolate/reject her, which will make building friendships difficult.

15. Emotional and social development in adolescence

Suggested answers could include:
- At the age of 15, James is likely to be experiencing puberty. Hormonal changes may cause mood swings, so he will be less able to cope with his emotions.
- The physical changes that are happening could cause him to become less confident about his appearance.
- Because James had poor exam results, his confidence in his own ability may be reduced and this may affect his self-esteem.
- If James cannot go on to college, it may prevent him from meeting new friends.

16. Emotional and social development in adulthood

Suggested answers could include:
Emotional development
- Anita's self-esteem may be affected because she no longer has a job.
- Anita may lose her independence because she is not working.

Social development
- It may damage Anita's relationship with Eryk, as she had to move away from family and friends because of his job.
- Anita may lose social contact with others because she does not know anyone.

Learning aim B

17. Genetic inheritance

Suggested answers could include:
- **Physical development:** a person's build and other athletic characteristics are inherited.
- **Emotional development:** appearance may affect how people feel about themselves.
- **Social development (linked to emotional development):** appearance may influence how a person feels about themselves and therefore their ability to socialise and make friends.

- **Intellectual development:** talents such as creativity may be passed down from parents.

18. Lifestyle choices

- Alice's ability to remember things and solve problems is likely to be affected, so she may make mistakes at work and may even lose her job.
- Her relationships with family and some friends could break down because of her drug-taking, which could affect her confidence and ability to build relationships in the future.

19. Illness and disease

B He has missed time at school

20. The influence of play

Suggested answers could include:

- The children will speak and listen to each other, so they will develop their language skills.
- The children will build friendships with one another when they play and therefore develop their social skills.
- The children may have to take turns with dressing-up clothes, so they will learn to share/moral development.
- The children will need to manipulate the toy instruments, so they will develop fine motor skills.

21. Culture

Suggested answers could include:

- Amy may become socially isolated.
- She may feel depressed.
- She may feel less secure.
- She may feel less contented.

22. Gender

Suggested answers could include:

- Pawel may develop low self-esteem because he feels he has failed.
- He will not have the opportunity to develop new intellectual skills.
- He may have a negative self-image if he compares himself with the person who got the job.
- Pawel's relationships with colleagues may change, because he feels that he has been discriminated against.

23. Role models and social isolation

Suggested answers could include:

- Wardell will not be able to build new relationships.
- He may feel less secure.
- It may affect his self-esteem.
- He may lose some ability to think creatively/problem solve.
- He may feel less contented with life.

24. Economic factors

- The status of a person's job may lead to a positive or negative self-image, as they may compare themselves with others.
- The status of employment may affect the level of pay, which can then affect a person's level of contentment and financial security.

25. Physical environment

C Len lives next to a very busy main road

26. Family relationships

Suggested answers could include:

- A feeling of security/contentment.
- Improved self-esteem.
- Positive self-image.

27. Friendships and relationships

Suggested answers could include:

- It may help him to become more confident/independent.
- He may develop friendship-building skills to enable him to develop other friendships.
- He may develop a positive self-image.
- He may feel more secure/contented.

28. Stress

Any two from the following: slows physical growth in children; delays the onset of puberty; speeds up the onset of the ageing process; can result in unhealthy eating, causing weight loss or gain.

29. Expected life events 1

An expected life event is an event that happens to most people during the course of their life.

30. Expected life events 2

Suggested answers could include:

- Drew achieved his degree.
- Drew has been offered a good job.
- Drew will have improved social status/more money from his job.

31. Unexpected life events 1

Darren – redundancy

Leanne – bereavement or illness

32. Unexpected life events 2

Suggested answers could include:

- Craig will lose his independence, because he can no longer make all his own decisions.
- It will affect his self-esteem negatively, because he can no longer work or continue with his usual lifestyle.
- Craig's social development will be affected, because he will not be able to continue his social relationships.
- He may feel upset and isolated, because he has little contact with his partner and friends.

33. Types of support

1 **Physical support** – supporting a person's mobility or physical health needs
   Emotional support – support to help people cope with their feelings
2 **Physical support** – help with mobility/dressing/personal care/help to become more independent
   Emotional support – help to understand illness/help to come to terms with illness/help to overcome stress/overcome depression

34. Managing change 1

Suggested answers could include:

Emotional development

- Mary may feel more safe and secure being back in her own home.
- She may feel more contented in a familiar setting.

Social development

- Mary will continue to have a strong relationship with Claire.
- She may have more independence in her own home.

35. Managing change 2

Suggested answers could include:

- help to cope with feelings because of bereavement
- advice/information about a specific illness
- someone to listen/reassure
- information or advice about redundancy/unemployment
- help with transport/mobility.

The following pages contain answers to the 'Now try this' questions in Unit 9 of the Revision Guide.

Learning aim A
40. Defining health and wellbeing
1 Emotional and intellectual
2 Holistic means looking at something as a whole and the definition of health and wellbeing covers all types of needs, so looks at the whole person.

41. Physical and intellectual factors
- To absorb facts, the opinions of others or instructions,
- To gain the knowledge, understanding and skills you need to succeed in life.

42. Emotional and social effects
By having the opportunities to mix with others, we can make and keep friendships and other relationships. Having an appropriate place to do this means we are comfortable and relaxed, can communicate effectively with each other and are kept safe.

43. Physical effects of an unhealthy lifestyle
It is important to have a healthy body fat composition because this keeps our body temperature regulated and our organs and tissues cushioned and insulated.

44. Intellectual effects of an unhealthy lifestyle
Any two from the following: her cold; her uncomfortable position; noise from the TV; the baby.

45. Emotional effects of an unhealthy lifestyle
Suggested answers could include:
- The dependence will mean that the person is being distracted by their cravings for the substance, so will not be concentrating on their partner's needs – for example, communicating with them properly.
- They may also smell of the substance, which may put their partner off, as could their behaviour and mood swings, their lack of money and their lifestyle.
- They may have poor self-esteem and low confidence because of the effects of the dependency on their body.

46. Social effects of an unhealthy lifestyle
- Zoltán will have mood swings and his behaviour may be aggressive, which may lead to arguments and cause conflict with family members.
- Zoltán's behaviour may embarrass his family in front of their friends.
- Zoltán may ask for money or steal from his family, causing more strain on family relationships.

47. Diet and nutrition
Eating too little can result in the body not consuming enough of the nutrients it needs – for example, not having enough protein to repair body cells and tissues.

48. Exercise
(a) $BMI = \frac{70}{1.6^2}$

$BMI = 27.3\,kg/m^2$

(b) Overweight.

49. Home environment
Suggested answers could include:
- Living somewhere clean and warm can lead to a person catching fewer illnesses and diseases.
- Living somewhere warm and comfortable with plenty of space allows a person to concentrate better when reading or studying.
- Better living conditions mean a person will be happier, because they feel comfortable and relaxed in nice surroundings.
- Better living conditions mean a person will not be ashamed to invite friends home and so extends their social opportunities.

50. Work environment
- A non-manual job may be sedentary, resulting in a lack of exercise.
- A non-manual job may be more stressful, leading to raised blood pressure and related health issues.

51. Alcohol consumption
Suggested answers could incude:
- Drinking too much alcohol can lead to liver damage, so Laura could develop liver diseases.
- Laura will experience cravings for alcohol when she is not drinking, which will lead to mood swings and feelings of unhappiness.
- She will also develop poor self-esteem as she will feel she is letting herself and others down by her inability to cut down.

52. Effects of alcohol
B Lung cancer

53. Smoking
- Alena may have started because: her friends did and she may want to feel accepted by the group.
- She has seen her parents or people in the media do it and thinks it makes her look more grown-up, cool or like a rebel.

54. Recreational drug use
One from: drugs can cause hallucinations; they can increase or decrease brain activity; they may change impressions of time and space; they may distort the senses to cause a person to hear and feel things that seem real but aren't, so making it hard to tell the difference between illusion and reality.

55. Sexual practices
- Contraction and spreading of STIs
- Unwanted pregnancy

56. Personal hygiene
Poor personal hygiene may result in a person contracting a disease or infection such as athlete's foot or diarrhoea, and also loss of friends and even social isolation.

57. Sleep patterns
Suggested answers could include:
- Gives time for the body to carry out biological maintenance tasks.
- Helps body function better the next day.
- Increases energy levels.
- Increases mental sharpness.

58. Influences on lifestyles 1
Suggested answers could include:
- Only allowing them to eat certain foods.
- Only letting them dress in a particular way.

59. Influences on lifestyles 2
C Pressure from other members of a social group to act in a certain way

60. Influences on lifestyles 3

The media can influence a person to lead an unhealthy lifestyle by portraying the ideal female body as being very slim, or by advertising showing that it's 'cool' to drink lots of alcohol or tempting them to eat fast food.

61. Influences on lifestyles 4

- They may not have been taught or not be aware of the risks of, for example, eating an unbalanced diet.
- They may not understand the risks, such as how poor hygiene can spread germs.

Learning aim B

62. Improving health and wellbeing 1

D I want to get fit so that I can do a 10k fun run on 21 May next year

63. Improving health and wellbeing 2

1 Franco could see a NHS stop smoking adviser. They would advise him on strategies he could use to help him stop, and give him alternative strategies and support and encouragement if he struggles during the first few weeks.

2 To cut down to 20 cigarettes a day in two weeks.

64. Improving health and wellbeing 3

- Gillie could record how much money she is saving each time she doesn't have a drink and look at the running total when she has a craving. This will remind herself of the treats she will be able to buy if she stays on her plan.
- Gillie could have a list of the health benefits of stopping drinking, including pictures of a healthy and unhealthy liver, to look at when she is wavering.

65. Improving health and wellbeing 4

'Cut down the number of tablets I take by half in eight weeks' time'.

This is SMART because it is specific (clear), measurable (cut down by half), achievable, realistic and time-related (in eight weeks).

66. Improving health and wellbeing 5

- The benefits give motivation to start a health plan.
- The benefits are a reminder of why it is important both to stick to the health plan when tempted to give up and to maintain the healthier lifestyle when the goal is achieved.

67. Improving health and wellbeing 6

One intervention strategy for reducing alcohol consumption is to order a soft drink every other drink when out socially. This helps because it halves the quantity of alcohol consumed while the person is still enjoying a drink every other round, so doesn't feel as though they are missing out so much.

68. Formal support

- A teacher can inform young people about the risks of having unprotected sex and the benefits of safer sex in a citizenship lesson.
- A teacher can refer a young person to other sources of support such as the school nurse or a formal support group if they have any concerns, such as being worried about the possibility of being pregnant or having caught a STI after unsafe sex at a party after drinking alcohol.

69. Informal support

If a person wanted to lose weight, they could access formal support by visiting their GP and being referred to a dietician, who will have been trained and paid to give the support. The person can ask their family members to give them informal support by also eating healthily and reminding them of why they want to lose weight when they are tempted to eat something unhealthy. Their family members are not paid or trained to give this support, but will still be able to help.

70. Support in maintaining positive change

- If someone wants to get more exercise, a friend could give support by joining a gym or fitness class with them, using the time where they might normally go for a drink to get fitter instead.
- A friend or family member could go for a run or a cycle ride with them, so they have company and are less likely to give up.

71. Barriers to health 1

- Shamma could go to the cinema or theatre with her friends instead of eating and drinking with them.
- Shamma could ask her doctor for advice on what exercise she can manage to do with her mobility problems, and then make sure she does some every day.

72. Barriers to health 2

- Cravings for the effects provided by the drugs due to their addictive nature.
- Peer group pressure – the temptation to join in when friends take recreational drugs.

73. Barriers to health 3

- Misha finds it hard to find motivation to make the changes needed because he feels more confident and relaxed when he drinks, and this is what makes it possible for him to socialise with his friends.
- Misha finds it hard to find motivation because he looks in the mirror and doesn't like what he sees, so doesn't think he can change or is worth the effort of changing.

74. Barriers to health 4

- Kristina's addiction means that she spends all her money on drugs and so cannot afford to eat as healthily as she could or join a gym to get fitter.
- Kristina's addiction means that she craves drugs, so even though she knows she needs to adopt a healthier lifestyle, she will find it very hard to resist the cravings, and will worry about the pain involved if she does try to give up.

75. Exam skills 1

No answers needed.

76. Exam skills 2

(a) $BMI = \dfrac{80}{1.7^2}$

$BMI = 27.7 \text{ kg/m}^2$

(b) **C** Oveweight

77. Exam skills 3

They could tell Kylie they don't like her smoking and voice their disapproval whenever she smokes, saying they don't want to passive smoke. They could also tell her that the smoking is making her clothes, hair and breath smell, which isn't nice for them. This will be a good incentive, because she probably wants to be accepted as part of the group.

They could help her give up by distracting her at times when she most wants a cigarette, suggesting alternative activities where she can't smoke or where she needs the money she would normally spend on cigarettes.

78. Exam skills 4

No answers needed.

Your own notes

Revision is more than just this Guide!

You can get even more practice on each topic you revise with our corresponding Revision Workbook.

1-to-1 page match with this Revision Guide.

Guided questions help build your confidence.

Questions get you ready for your assessment test.

UNIT 1
Learning aim B

Had a go ☐ Nearly there ☐ Nailed it! ☐

The influence of play

1 The following information is about Madge.
Read the information and answer the questions below.

Madge is a child-minder. She cares for three children: Amir aged 7, Humayra aged 4, and Timmy, who is 12 months. Timmy enjoys puppet play.

(a) Which aspect of language development is puppet play **most** important for?

(1 mark)

Put a cross in **one** box ☒ to indicate your answer.

A ☐ Memory and recall   B ☐ Speech and vocabulary

C ☐ Problem solving   D ☐ Creative thinking

Timmy enjoys solitary play. Amir and Humayra like to take part in social play.

> Guided

(b) Outline the difference between 'solitary play' and 'social play'.   (2 marks)

In solitary play, children play alone or alongside others, but in social play, they ....

....

Madge wants to provide activities that will promote each child's emotional development.

(c) For **each** child, give an example of an activity that could be used to promote their emotional development.   (3 marks)

Complete the table below.

Child	Activity
Amir	
Humayra	
Timmy	

20

Sample page from Revise BTEC
Health and Social Care Revision Workbook

Hints will help you prepare for this topic in your assessment test.

Get ready for the test by completing our practice assessment test.

Check out the matching Revision Workbook

Revise BTEC First in Health and Social Care Revision Workbook
978 1 4469 0982 9